Buyig Solo

Buying Solo

The Single Woman's Guide
to Buying a First Home

Vanessa Summers

A PERIGEE BOOK

A Perigee Book
Published by the Penguin Group
Penguin Group (USA) Inc.
375 Hudson Street, New York, New York 10014, USA
Penguin Group (Canada), 10 Alcorn Avenue, Toronto, Ontario M4V 3B2, Canada
(a division of Pearson Penguin Canada Inc.)
Penguin Books Ltd., 80 Strand, London WC2R 0RL, England
Penguin Group Ireland, 25 St. Stephen's Green, Dublin 2, Ireland (a division of Penguin Books Ltd.)
Penguin Group (Australia), 250 Camberwell Road, Camberwell, Victoria 3124, Australia
(a division of Pearson Australia Group Pty. Ltd.)
Penguin Books India Pvt. Ltd., 11 Community Centre, Panchsheel Park, New Delhi—110 017, India
Penguin Group (NZ), cnr. Airborne and Rosedale Roads, Albany, Auckland 1310, New Zealand
(a division of Pearson New Zealand Ltd.)
Penguin Books (South Africa) (Pty.) Ltd., 24 Sturdee Avenue, Rosebank, Johannesburg 2196, South Africa

Penguin Books Ltd., Registered Offices: 80 Strand, London WC2R 0RL, England

PRINTING HISTORY
Perigee trade paperback edition / March 2005

PERIGEE is a registered trademark of Penguin Group (USA) Inc.
The "P" design is a trademark belonging to Penguin Group (USA) Inc.

Library of Congress Cataloging-in-Publication Information

Summers, Vanessa, 1971–
    Buying solo : the single woman's guide to buying a first home / Vanessa Summers.
        p. cm.
    ISBN 0-399-53076-2 (pbk.)
    1. House buying—United States—Handbooks, manuals, etc. 2. Mortgage loans—United States—
Handbooks, manuals, etc. 3. Single women—United States—Economic conditions. I. Title.

HD259.S87 2005
643'.12'08652—dc22   2004052934

PRINTED IN THE UNITED STATES OF AMERICA

10   9   8   7   6   5   4   3   2   1

to my extraordinary life partner, Andor . . .
my only wish is to come home to you.
actually, there is no time that i am not already home with you.
my forever friend.
i love you.

Contents

Introduction

The best investment on earth is earth.
—*Louis J. Glickman, real estate investor*

Congratulations! If you are motivated enough to pick up a copy of this book, you are interested in exploring the possibility of buying your own home. Getting into the real estate market is a huge step. It's a challenge, it's a lot of work, it can be scary . . . and it's also one of the smartest, most empowering things you can do for yourself. Knowledge is power—and you are smart to equip yourself with all the how-to's before entering into this exciting adventure! This book will show you how to do it.

Buying a first home may seem incredibly overwhelming and even somewhat daunting to you. You may be thinking: *Am I ready for this? Are my finances ready for this?* And, especially, *Can I really do this on my own?*

The first step: relax. We're going to get through this

together. In addition to being a registered financial adviser and a licensed stockbroker, I'm also your peer. As a recent homebuyer myself, I faced all these questions and more as I embarked on the adventure of buying my first home. My motivation for writing this book was born out of my passion to inspire other young women to believe that it is truly possible to be a homeowner today—with or without a husband, boyfriend, or partner. In fact, it's not just possible, it's *essential*.

If you're reading this book, you probably have at least a few goals for your future—financial and otherwise. You have a job, but you anticipate finding an even better one in the near future. You make enough money, but you plan to make more. You want to find the right person to spend the rest of your life with . . . but, in the meantime, you don't want to put your current life on hold. You want to build more wealth and financial security, but you're not sure how to start.

Congratulations! You're on your way to achieving all of these goals. The fact is, **buying a home is the single best investment a woman can make**—on her own or in tandem with someone else. I'm going to show you how.

Why a Special Book for Single Women?

This is a question that I've heard from a lot of people since starting this book. The truth is, there are specific concerns women face when buying property that just don't come up for most men or couples—most are more psychological than monetary. *Shouldn't I just wait until I "settle down" a bit more before I buy a place of my own? Can I still afford to live my life the way I want to with a mortgage hanging over my head? Can I even scrape together enough for a down payment on a piece of property? Shouldn't I just wait until I find a partner so I can buy a place that's big enough to "grow" into?*

When I went looking for a book to help me out on my personal quest to own, I was shocked at the hole on the real estate bookshelf. Although there are lots of books and articles that cover the topic of buying real estate, few are geared toward the single, solvent-but-not-loaded young woman who is trying to break into it for the first time. As a stockbroker and financial adviser, I'm no novice when it comes to money and investing. But these other books left me cold. I could understand their advice, and some of it was helpful. But I just didn't feel like it related to me.

This book is an instruction guide for the single, young woman (or at least the young at heart) that breaks down the process of buying your first home into an achievable, motivational, and [gasp] even *fun* process. You'll learn why home ownership is such a great investment option to explore right now, all the many creative ways to address credit concerns and down-payment fears, and easy-to-follow steps of action to take in finding and buying your first home!

Always bear in mind that your own resolution to succeed is more important than any other thing.
—Abraham Lincoln

A "Friend" in the Business

Courteney Cox, the famous *Friends* star, is on her seventh house and has made a second career out of buying, rehabbing, and selling property. Courteney revealed that when she bought her first house back in the late 1980s, she was flat broke. But, as she got more money and built up her home equity, she changed houses—in effect, upgrading.

When asked if the price tag and commitment involved in buying her very first house made her nervous, Courteney replied, "It was something I thought I couldn't or shouldn't afford. First it was *couldn't*, and then it was *shouldn't*." But while talking with some successful colleagues about the ups and downs of investing, she realized that real estate was a smart (and fun) place to devote her money and her energy. One of her more recent purchases has been reported to be an estimated $10,000,000 Malibu beachfront property.

Can I Really Afford to Buy on My Own?

The short answer? Yes. Look around you—in 2003, single women purchased 21 percent of all homes sold. That's a lot of sisters doing it for themselves.

Think of it this way: As of this writing, approximately 10 percent of all homes in America are for sale. That's a whopping seven million homes of all prices, locations, and conditions, including: one-hundred-year-old properties, brand-new homes, single-family homes, co-ops, and condos. Of these homes, some are single-story structures, while others are in high-rise buildings. Some are in rural areas, while others are in the city. Prices can range from a few thousand to the millions. Granted, some areas of the U.S. (major metropolitan areas like New York, Boston, and Los Angeles especially) can be more expensive and challenging, but there really are all sorts of properties to choose from if you're willing to broaden your definition of what you're looking for. If you really want to buy a home, and you think you can't afford it, the likelihood is that you are wrong in your assumption.

You see things; and you say, "Why?" But I dream things that never were; and I say, "Why Not?!"
—*George Bernard Shaw*

Mario Manzanilla, mortgage consultant at Kennedy Capital Management (www.kennedycapital.com) was recently quoted as saying, "I have been in real estate for more than three decades, and I've seen people in all sorts of financial condition buy homes. I've seen people in bankruptcy purchase property. I've seen people with absolutely no money, and terrible credit history, buy homes. I've even seen people who are unemployed purchase a house."

OK, so these people may not have been able to buy a house in Beverly Hills, but they did make good on a home purchase. If you are legally able to enter into a contract, you should be able to buy a home. With all the options out there, if you really want to buy a home, there is probably something that you can afford, no matter what your financial condition.

Some of the most important real estate topics we'll cover in this book include:

- Why the time to buy your first home is NOW.

- How mortgages actually work, and how much monthly mortgage you can truly afford to pay.

- How to make your credit history "real estate ready"—or even buy your first home with bad credit.

- How to buy with little or no money down payment.

- How to find the right mortgage broker and mortgage for you.

- How to find a real estate broker you can actually do business with.

- Where to find the best deals in every location.

- How to actually make an offer and negotiate like Donald Trump.

Once you learn the "real deal" about the real estate market, buying your first home solo can become a reality—so keep reading!

The Time Is Now!

The Most Common Excuses That Stop Single Women from Buying a Home . . . And Why You Should Do It Anyway

Question: How do I become an optimist?
Answer: Proper preparation and attention to details.
—*Coach John R. Wooden,*
former UCLA basketball coach

Lately, all Joelle can think about is getting out of the rental trap. Her landlord took two months to repair a leak in her apartment earlier this year, and it looks like he's going to raise the rent again next month. Her friend Meg just bought a place of her own, a little apartment not far from Joelle, and it's really got Joelle thinking about whether that step might be right for her, too.

But when it comes to buying a place of her own, Joelle just doesn't know where to begin, or even if she's quite ready. She's smart, single, almost thirty, with a solid job as an editor at a large magazine. She's quite good at her job and has every hope that she'll continue to advance in responsibility and pay . . . but at present she doesn't have much extra cash *after she pays her bills each month. Sometimes it's a struggle just making the payments on her credit card. But she just inherited a small amount of money from her grandmother, and she thinks it might be enough for a down payment . . . if she plays her cards right.*

Complicating matters is Joelle's boyfriend, Ian. They've been dating about a year, and they're definitely serious . . . but they've discussed the issue of moving in together and both agree that they're not quite ready yet.

Joelle's been scouring the real estate pages, and she just saw a great place that she loves. She knows that getting her own place is a great investment, but still her uncertainties persist. Can she swing a mortgage payment each month? Does she really want that kind of responsibility? And if she does go ahead and buy this place herself, what does that mean for her relationship with Ian?

* * *

Think about it . . . you, a homeowner! No longer will your monthly rent be paying money toward someone else's real estate investment; you'll be paying money to yourself. Owning your home is all about putting yourself first and thinking proactively about your future. It's a statement to the rest of the world (and to yourself!) that you're smart, independent, and able to take care of yourself. It lets others in both your personal and professional life know that you are responsible when it comes to taking care of your financial life, and proactive about planning your future.

But many single women are somewhat reluctant to buy, for a variety of reasons (both actual and psychological). Let's look at some of those reasons.

"I Can't Afford to Buy."

As women, we generally know what we can afford when it comes to bargain hunting for discount designer shoes, a cheap plane ticket to a best friend's wedding, or even a forced $100 monthly contribution from our paycheck into a tax-deductible 401(k). However, when it comes to a big-ticket purchase, such as buying our first home, we are left dazed and confused. Why? Well, to begin with, we don't have a lot of historical role models to look to. Our mothers probably bought their first homes in conjunction with a husband. We are truly the first generation of young single women who have the means (and the urge) to own a piece of the Great American Dream, even before the Great American Dream man appears in our lives!

I grew up with a fantastic mother who always told me as a young girl: "It is just as easy to fall in love with a rich man as it is a poor man!" It's an old-fashioned sentiment, but a lot of women our age still seem to believe it. In fact, in a recent OppenheimerFunds survey of single Gen X women, more than 70 percent of the young women polled believed that their financial future plans would begin officially when they settled down with a partner.

But more and more, women are starting to realize that planning for their financial futures starts *now*, not when they meet Mr. Right. We're not gambling that we'll find someone who can give us all the things we want—we're earning them ourselves. Where do you see yourself in a couple of years? Having more responsibility? Making more money? Feeling more secure in your professional life? If you're curious enough to pick up this book, I think the answer is probably "yes." You will most likely be more financially stable in a few years, have built up some good home equity in your first home, and be ready to trade up in (rather than just break in) the home-buying marketplace! The time to get into the game is now.

If you are currently paying a few hundred dollars to a thousand dollars or more per month in rent, you could be paying less each month to own a home. Check out this theoretical chart that may help refocus your vision on how the system truly works. This chart shows you how expensive a home you can actually afford based on your current monthly rent that you are paying. Simply follow the calculation:

Take your monthly rent and multiply by
200 = Theoretical purchase price of first home

CURRENT MONTHLY RENT   ESTIMATED FUTURE FIRST
                              HOME PRICE

$_____ per month x 200 = $_____

EXAMPLE:
$ 750 per month x 200 = $ 150,000

If you are paying $750 per month in rent, then you could approximate with the chart above—at the current interest rate level of approximately 6 percent—that you would be paying the same amount per month to actually own a $150,000 home (note—this amount includes tax savings). All of a sudden your monthly rent doesn't sound so cheap anymore, does it? Maybe you can't afford *not* to buy.

"I'm Not Sure How Long I Want to Live in One Place."

Good, because no one else is ever truly sure about this! Statistics from the National Association of Realtors (NAR) reveal that nowadays renters and homeowners live in their homes only about five to seven years, on average. Plus, appreciation in your home's value will create amazing *equity* (the difference between the market value of your home and the actual amount you owe on your mortgage) for you that can be incredibly useful in the future. Building equity is a smart way for you to increase your net worth, but there's more to it than that. You can use that equity to trade up to a bigger home, start a business, go back to school, or even travel around the world for a year! There are no guarantees that your home will increase in value at all, but remember that statistic about home prices increasing on average 3–5 percent per annum— and in big metropolitan cities that number tends to be much higher.

What you can be sure about is this: The average American woman will make $25,000 per year over the course of her professional life (forty years), for a total of $1,000,000! Yet, at the end of our working lives, many of us will have debt and no retirement savings to show for it. You, as a young woman, get the superb opportunity to begin the quickest and easiest way to achieving the lifestyle and financial freedom of your dreams by making your first property purchase today—regardless of how long you may (or may not) want to live in one place! Did you know that the average non-home-owning American's net worth is $1,930 . . . while a homeowner's net worth is estimated at $63,000!

"I Don't Have Enough Money for a Down Payment."

As of this writing, we are in a booming real estate marketplace, due to low interest rates and robust appreciation of house prices. The old paradigms that once existed when buying a home—a big down payment of 20 percent or more, an amazing credit report, and a big-bucks job—are no longer necessary.

In fact, mortgage lenders have learned over time that the percentage difference of default to loan ratio for homebuyers with great credit, incomes, and a huge down payment vs. individuals with not-so-great credit, minimal incomes carrying debt balances, with no down payments was fractional. Meaning, the risk factor for mortgage lenders to offer home loans to us single gals, who may not have a perfect credit record is not a problem. They still want our business in a big way.

"I Want to Wait to Buy Until I Have a Family of My Own."

When you are in your twenties and thirties, you may not be thinking much about buying your starter or first home. In fact, many single women are reluctant to buy a small house or apartment because they fear that they'll soon "outgrow" it when they one day meet a partner or have a family. As a young woman, you must equip yourself with the facts: we will out-live men by seven to ten years and earn approximately 25 percent less, plus spend an average of eleven years out of the workplace due to child rearing and the care of elderly parents. This adds up to greater challenges to secure our long-term financial futures. As a young single woman, you will always need to empower yourself with regards to your finances—family or no family! Waiting to buy a home till you have a family is like waiting to exercise, eat healthy, and take good care of yourself till you meet your life partner. What is wrong with this picture? It doesn't work!

This is the dirty little secret for many single women looking to buy solo. We fear that, by buying a place that fits our life now, we're cutting off our options for the future. It is not unrealistic to think that within the next few years, you will hook-up with a special some-one whom you will want to share your life with. And it's also likely that what you can afford now as a sin-gle woman won't be quite enough space for two!

But, as we discussed earlier, you're actually *increas-ing* your options by buying solo, not limiting them. Forget for a minute the cost of owning your own home today—what about the future? As a renter, you most likely have already experienced the increased cost of living when your landlord has increased your rent payment each year due to inflation. Since inflation grows anywhere from 3–5 percent per year, let's take into consideration that inflation will be 4 percent per year. The following chart illustrates what will happen to that $750 rental cost per month in the future due to inflation.

RENTAL INCREASE OVER TIME DUE TO INFLATION

TODAY	$750
10 YEARS	$1095
20 YEARS	$1620
30 YEARS	$2400
40 YEARS	$3550
50 YEARS	$5260

Note: Your rent will increase this much in this many years due to inflation!

Remember from the example earlier, that paying $750 in rent is roughly equivalent to buying a home for $150,000. Think of it this way, when you take inflation into consideration at 4 percent growth per year, in thirty years your $750 a month in rent will be a gigantic $2,400 per month. That would be the equivalent of buying a house for about $600,000!

In order to get a truly accurate read for yourself of what might happen to your current rent due to the annual inflation issue, take a look at the chart below and plug in a few numbers:

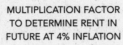

	MULTIPLICATION FACTOR TO DETERMINE RENT IN FUTURE AT 4% INFLATION	

YOUR CURRENT MONTHLY RENT		PROJECTED FUTURE RENT YEARS
$_____	x 1.48 =	_____ in 10 years
$_____	x 2.19 =	_____ in 20 years
$_____	x 3.24 =	_____ in 30 years
$_____	x 4.80 =	_____ in 40 years
$_____	x 7.11 =	_____ in 50 years
$_____	x 10.52 =	_____ in 60 years

Keep in mind, too, that even though the cost of purchasing a home increases over the years, the majority of your housing costs are not exposed to inflation. In fact the government offers you significant savings due to your tax-deductible interest payments to your mortgage, which we will discuss more at length later in this chapter.

The concept here is basic: You will always need a place to live. Over the long haul, you can count on inflation—so it is in your best interest (no pun intended) to do the homework and buy even a little starter home today. The idea is that if you are in your twenties or thirties, you will most likely own several homes in your lifetime. It is not unreasonable to think that you will move more than four, five, or more times. This doesn't have to be about buying your dream house from the get-go (that may be three or four houses down the road), as much as it is about buying a solid home that you will be able to sell when you want—most likely in the next few years. You can then trade up to a bigger house in a better neighborhood. The fact is, if you get started on your own, you are that much closer to being able to buy a house that's big enough for the two of you when you find Mr. Right . . . and Junior, too, when he comes along!

You see, in getting the ball rolling with your first purchase of a home, you are opening yourself up to many wonderful wealth-building opportunities. And, as a side note, women who stop waiting to find the right "someone" to buy with and start taking charge of their own lives may suddenly find themselves even more appealing! One woman recently confided in me: "Once I bought my first condo, I met my future husband within months. It was the best choice I could have made to ensure attracting a fantastic partner!" Owning our own financial power means owning our own opportunity to attract the best possible partner for the future family we envision for ourselves.

The Joys of Home Ownership

So, why now? Sure, we've all heard the stories on the nightly news breathlessly reporting the rise and fall of interest rates, the plunging stock market, and the escalating price of real estate. You probably know by now that real estate is a good place to put your money. But there are several real advantages to owning your own place.

No More Landlords!

Consider it—you will finally be free to decorate, paint, and fix up a home to your personal liking without getting your landlord's approval first. Once, when I was still renting, I painted my kitchen a gloriously bright hue my roommate and I dubbed "Lose-Your-Deposit Orange." It was a great color . . . and we paid for it when we moved out.

Plus, say goodbye to landlords who are slow to make improvements on your home or fix problems. When you own, you're your own landlord! Write yourself a nasty note to fix that leaky faucet.

More Security for the Future

Even the kindest landlord needs to raise the rent once in a while. And most raise it more often than that. When you rent, you're always at the mercy of someone else, who may decide he can get double for that tiny studio you're crammed into for an exorbitant monthly fee. When you buy and you get a fixed-rate mortgage, that cost will remain at the same rate even as rents rise.

Saying *"hasta la vista"* to landlords also keeps you from running the risk of renting places that the landlord may decide to sell.

Home Equity Rules!

Your home equity is the difference between your out-standing loan on your home (the mortgage) and the market value of your home. Say you have a mortgage on your first home of $200,000, and your current appraisal for your home is approximated at $250,000. In this case, your home equity would be $50,000. EASY! By owning a home and paying down on the mortgage on your home (instead of paying that money in rent) over the years, you create equity. And, in the event that your home does not appreciate in value (a slim chance), you will still be creating equity while you pay down the mortgage. That is why your home is an investment opportunity.

A single woman in a recent workshop I led, who works as a director/producer in Los Angeles, was lucky enough two years ago to have her father help her buy a building of four apartments in the trendy Venice neighborhood. She lives in one and rents the rest. She just had her property appraised and found it has doubled in value in just two years!

Let's pretend that you end up being one of those rare people who owns a home and doesn't see any appreciation in your home's market value. Even in this worst-case scenario, you will still benefit by paying down the remaining due on your mortgage. In other words, one day you'll own the home free-and-clear. Retirees often boast of the great financial joys of being free of mortgage payments.

Another great upside to building equity by owning a home is that it offers you multiple financing options, which you can explore at some point in the future for education, travel, starting a business, remodeling your home, or financing your retirement. Think of your home as your forced savings account, where you automatically deposit X dollars every month. And, though it's best to wait a few years before doing this, you can also withdraw funds from your "savings account" if needed. By borrowing through your home's equity, you can tap a low-cost source of cash—since the interest you pay on the mortgage of your home is generally tax-deductible (which we will discuss later in this chapter).

A final way to tap into your home's equity is to "trade down" or "trade out" to cash in on major tax-free gains! That is, you may choose to sell a $200,000 home and replace it with one costing $100,000—hence, freeing up $100,000 in capital. The Internal Revenue Service allows that if you have owned and lived in your primary residence for a total of two of the past five years, you qualify for up to $250,000 in tax-free profits. Couples can take as much as $500,000. In fact, before Congress passed this law in 1997 by revising IRC 121, the law required that sellers either buy a more expensive home or pay taxes on the difference. As one certified public accountant was quoted as saying, "There is nothing else like home ownership from a tax-savings standpoint! If you qualify, jump on it like there's no tomorrow."

Huge Tax Write-off Advantages

There are two basic expenditures to consider when buying your own home: the down payment (plus closing expenses) and the monthly mortgage pay-

The Equity Advantage

Oprah Winfrey—you know, the most famous and mega-rich talk-show host ever—is currently estimated to be worth $1 billion dollars . . . and she knows a thing or two about building some serious home equity.

Jeff Jacobs, president of Oprah's Harpo Entertainment, in Chicago, and her appointed strategic adviser, was interviewed for a *Fortune* magazine cover story featuring Oprah. In the article, Jeff revealed that one of the key reasons why Oprah is so wealthy is that she understood early on that it is not just about how much you make, but how much you keep of what you make. Oprah recently purchased one of the most expensive properties ever—a $55 million beachfront mansion in Montecito, California. Not bad for a girl who started from extremely humble beginnings! Imagine what is available to you, right now, today!

Clearly, Oprah knows that equity-building is a fantastic path to keeping and making more of what you make.

---

ments. Many women figure they could swing a monthly mortgage payment, but the thought of scraping together 10 or 20 percent of the purchase price for a down payment is daunting. We'll talk more about the "down-payment myth" in the next chapter—there are many liberal loans and financing opportunities these days to help those of us who don't have a big chunk of cash handy to use as a down payment on a home. But it's those monthly payments that offer the big tax advantages that every homeowner raves about come April 15 each year.

Interest Deductions

Here's the deal: Homeowners (except those in the very top tax brackets) can deduct a percentage of their mortgage interest (up to a $1,000,000 loan) and property taxes from their ordinary income. This adds up to some serious savings. You see, if you look at an amortization schedule on any home loan, you will see that in the first five to seven years, almost 95 percent of your payments each month go toward servicing the interest you are paying on your mortgage. That is why for the first several years you own your home, you're getting some big tax breaks at the end of each year. In effect, the amount of initial monthly payments is much less than it seems, as the actual cost becomes much less to you in the bigger picture due to what you save on your taxes each year.

Let's say that your mortgage is $1,000 a month and is broken down as follows:

Principal	$35
Interest	$835
Taxes	$100
Insurance	$30
Total	**$1,000**

What does this mean on your 1040 tax returns? If you were in the 28 percent tax bracket, since you get to deduct the interest and taxes from your regular income, you get a whopping $935 a month tax deduction. That is a cash savings of $262 per month when all is said and done. Not to shabby.

Hence, when you take into consideration the monthly

tax savings on your mortgage payment, your actual cost is significantly lower. In the example above, you save almost a third in real dollars cost to you. Instead of the payment being $1,000 a month, after all is tallied up your real after-tax cost becomes $738 per month. The bottom line is that with a monthly mortgage payment, you not only create the opportunity to build great home equity for yourself over time, you also get the opportunity to save a real chunk of change that would have normally been paid out in taxes from your gross income.

Well that's great, you may be thinking. *I'll get more than $3,000 back at the end of the year when I do my taxes. But I still have to write that big mortgage check every month.* The good news is that your company's payroll can accommodate you on this. Your employer can actually anticipate what your monthly tax savings will be and add this amount back into your paycheck—in effect, this means you're hanging on to your extra money each pay period instead of loaning it to Uncle Sam for the year. (Check with your accountant or tax adviser, who can help you review what your allowable deductions will be and determine how your paycheck should be adjusted.) In the preceding example, it is possible to have $262 added back into your monthly paycheck. Keep in mind: You would still be writing a $1,000 check to the bank each month, but you'd also have less money withheld from each paycheck, so you'd have more money to use to pay your mortgage. All you need to do is instruct your employer to include additional deductions up to the allowable amount for your interest and property tax.

Home Improvement Deductions

So, what if you buy a new home and it needs a new roof in a few years? Sure, it's a pain, but there's good news, too—that roof is also tax deductible. But you'll have to wait until you sell to reap the benefits. The IRS allows you to exclude from taxation that portion of your profit that was due to capital improvements. In effect, the government allows you to add the cost of improvements at point of sale of your home to your original purchase price.

It is important to note that only *capital improvement* costs qualify for this special tax law, not *maintenance and repair expenses*. What is the difference? Capital improvements include things that you do to your home that permanently increase the value and lengthen the life, such as improvements to the landscaping, appliances, heater, roof, remodeling, etc. Maintenance and repair expenses include the fix-it-up items, such as fixing leaky faucets, painting, lawn mowing, etc.

The bigger picture here is that the tax incentives you receive when it comes to owning property are one of the most attractive features about the entire home-owning process, as the government offers many truly attractive cost-cutting opportunities to make this investment vehicle one that you should not miss out on!

Leverage

The final word on why "The Time Is Now" when it comes to buying your first home has to do with the simple mathematics of investing. You see, with a real estate purchase you have the opportunity to create amazing wealth with very little or nothing down.

Think about this for a moment. If you buy a $100,000 house with $10,000 as a down payment, and the house appreciates in value to $110,000, you have effectively recouped your initial investment of $10,000 you put down to own a home worth $100,000.

Robert Kiyosaki wrote a bestselling book called *Rich Dad, Poor Dad*. He has many powerful ideas when it comes to money and building wealth, one of which addresses being an "Indian Giver" when it comes to investing. His point being, you want to make sure you get your original investment back, the sooner the better. In the preceding example, you have accomplished just that! You recouped your $10,000 investment and now own a $100,000 investment— not too shabby. Remember, home values in all locations have always gone through up-and-down cycles. However, over the long haul property values almost always appreciate, and the increases are usually far greater than the declines. So, if you have a long-term (ideally a decade or more) investing-time horizon, you should do just fine if you invest in real estate. The biggest mistake you could be making is not buying!

> *Are you in earnest? Then seize this very minute.*
> *Whatever you can do, or dream you can, begin it.*
> *Boldness has genius, power, and magic in it. Only engage*
> *and then the mind grows healed; only begin, and then*
> *the goal will be completed.*
> —*Johann Wolfgang von Goethe*

The best time to buy a house is always a decade ago. A decade from now, today's prices may look dirt-cheap. Take a look at the following chart:

SINGLE-FAMILY AVERAGE MEDIAN HOME PRICES
IN THE UNITED STATES (1963–2003)

Year	Median Price	Percentage Increase
1963	$19,000	—
1973	$25,000	32%
1983	$65,000	160%
1993	$120,000	85%
2003	$180,000	50%
2013	$355,000	97% (Future Price Prediction)

*Source: Dr. Marshall Reddik / California Association of Realtors

In conclusion, you have multiple motivating factors to make buying your first home an amazing investment—in your future and in yourself. You don't have to be intimidated or afraid to buy solo. It's time to finally say goodbye to your landlord and embark upon your own real estate adventure. The rest of this book will show you how.

2

How Much House Can I Afford?

The Basics of Budgeting for a Mortgage

Look the world straight in the eye.
—Helen Keller

So, she's made the decision. Jenny, a pharmaceutical sales rep in the Midwest, has finally decided to stop renting and start looking for a place of her own to buy. She's been browsing the real estate section of the Sunday paper, looking at the houses and condos in her area, but the numbers don't mean anything to her. All she knows is that every house, even the cheapest, sounds like a lot. Too much.

"I know how much I pay every month in rent," she says, "but I don't know how that translates into a purchase price on a house. How do I know how much house I can really afford?"

* * *

The million-dollar question! As a first-time home buyer, this will be one of the most pressing questions you will need to figure out in order to have a happy, stress-free home-buying experience. Unless you're prepared to plunk down all cash for your home, your mortgage will typically be the greatest debt you'll ever owe . . . and probably the biggest expense of your life. It's scary stuff. But the good news is that getting a mortgage is also the best way to build equity and long-term financial independence.

Mortgage Mathematics Made Simple

A mortgage is simply a loan that you take out to help you finance the difference between the cash you have for the down payment of your first home and the actual purchase price of the home you are buying. Homes in your neck of the woods could be anywhere from a few thousand to $500,000 or more, and the fact is that most of us don't have that kind of change available in our bank accounts to draw upon—hence, the mortgage.

> *To be successful, keep looking tanned, live in an*
> *elegant building (even if you're in the cellar), be seen*
> *in smart restaurants (even if you nurse one drink),*
> *and if you borrow, borrow big.*
> —*Aristotle Onassis*

The standard practice is that mortgages require a monthly payment to repay them, or, technically speaking, to service your debt. Most mortgage payments are comprised of four elements, which we will review in more detail toward the end of this chapter. For now, just familiarize yourself with the acronym

PITI, representing the four elements that create your monthly mortgage payment.

1. **Principal:** Just as it probably sounds, it is your repayment of the original loan borrowed.

2. **Interest:** What your lender charges you for the use of the money borrowed.

3. **Taxes:** You will pay property taxes.

4. **Insurance:** Kind of like when you get a car, you are required to get coverage for a number of "what if" scenarios. With a house, *private mortgage insurance* (PMI) is required if you put less than 20 percent down on a home purchase.

A big mistake many people make when shopping for a first home is that they use generic formulas that mortgage lenders offer in calculating how much house they can afford. Yeah, like the ones that you find on real estate websites for free! Those generic Web mortgage calculators are, in fact, often poor barometers of what you can *really* afford when shopping for a home. Why? It is kind of like qualifying for a $10,000 limit on your credit card account. Just because you *qualify* for that $10,000 limit does not actually mean that you can afford to use the entire line of credit offered to you!

In the next chapter, we'll learn some of the specifics about what types of mortgages are available to you, and what additional costs are involved with securing this type of loan from a lender. But first, let's explore what will be a feasible financial fit for you when it comes to paying your monthly mortgage.

What Mortgage Companies Look At

There are a number of different things to take into consideration when it comes to securing a mortgage. The most surprising thing most first-time borrowers find is that what lenders will tell you is OK to borrow and what you can actually *afford* to borrow are sometimes two very different things. It's up to you, the person who will be writing those checks every month, to figure out your own financial goals, how much money you will need to achieve them, and where you are today. In essence, all mortgage lenders can do is tell you their specific criteria for approving and denying you a mortgage application and how they actually calculate the maximum that you're eligible to borrow.

So, what are the specific criteria, you ask? A mortgage lender calculates how much house you can afford by first looking at your before-tax income (also known as your *gross income*), your credit history, and how much outstanding debt you have to service each month. Depending on which lender you choose to do business with, a traditional lender will most likely tell you that your monthly mortgage payment cannot exceed 33 percent of your gross income, including debt.

What this means is that if you earn $6,300 per month and $300 of that per month goes to service your outstanding debts (such as student loans, auto loans, and credit card bills), you will be allowed to put 33 percent of $6,300 less your monthly $300 debt service payment. In this example, your maximum monthly mortgage allowable by this lender would be $1,800. Not quite sure this makes sense? Take a look at this table below:

Gross Monthly Income (GMI)	=	$6,300
Maximum Allowable Monthly Mortgage		
Payment is 33% of GMI	=	$2,100
Less Your Monthly Debt Service Payments	=	−$300
Total Maximum Monthly Mortgage Allowable	=	**$1,800**

But this 33 percent rule is just a guideline. Sometimes lenders will increase the maximum allowable percentage ratio of debt to GMI of your mortgage payment, up to 36, 40, or even 45 percent. Keep in mind, the rate of interest you may pay on these loans may be higher on these types of loans, due to the fact that the risk factor is higher for the lender. It all depends on the lender, the market, and your specific financial profile.

Sally was overly ambitious about getting a fantastic first home in a notoriously challenging city for first-time homebuyers—San Francisco! Sally had high expectations about finding a first home with pricey criteria that did not always match her budget—generous square footage and a large backyard for a garden.

Sally ended up purchasing her first home for $750,000—a whopping 30 percent over her realistic budget amount of $500,000. Currently, Sally spends the majority of her time each month stressing out about how she is going to make her mortgage payments—she has been late with payment three months in a row. She has borrowed money from several friends and family members to meet her mortgage payments since she purchased the house. In her own words, she feels her house has become her very own private prison cell.

Even though a lender may offer you a loan, it does not mean that it will be affordable for you given the overall snapshot of your financial picture at that time.

Prequalification vs. Preapproval

You have probably heard of these terms loosely, but it is important to know that there is a big difference between being *prequalified* and *preapproved*. When you're first starting to look for a home, it's a good idea to call up a few banks and/or mortgage brokers to see whether you prequalify for a loan. They will ask you a few questions, give your "numbers" a preliminary review, and guesstimate how much you can afford to spend on a home. It's a good benchmark for you as you're starting to look at property—if you're prequalified for $150,000, and all the houses in your dream neighborhood are going for half a million, you might need to broaden your search parameters a bit. On the other hand, a prequalification is not a guarantee from a lender. Just because you are prequalified for a mortgage does NOT mean you're preapproved.

The preapproval process is more rigorous, but also more helpful to both you and a seller. With preapproval, a bank or mortgage broker takes a thorough look at how much you earn, owe, and have in your bank account. The broker will give your financial snapshot a good review, they will then commit to you in writing that they will fund a loan on your behalf for a certain amount, pending a successful appraisal of the property you decide upon.

Equipping yourself with preapproval allows you to show prospective sellers that you are serious and that you have done your homework. In today's competitive housing market, it is important to put your best foot forward with the competition. Especially in "hot" real estate markets, offers can be made and accepted within days of a property going on the market. If you're not prequalified and ready to move quickly, you might miss out.

Why don't more people do the preapproval vs. prequalifying? Well, in order to get preapproved, you will need to shell out some cash. Prequalifying is a free process, while preapproval may cost you a couple hundred bucks. However, most lenders won't charge you this fee until you actually get the loan. And if you're serious about house hunting, it's a good investment to make.

The Interest Rate Game

One of the major reasons it is an amazing time for you, the first-time homebuyer to get into that first home has to do with the level of current interest rates. *Interest rates,* or the rate at which a lender will lend you money, impacts how much house you can afford in a huge way—making that possible first-time home purchase affordable or not!

If interest rates were at 8 percent (like they were in the late 1990s), you would probably only be able to afford a house that is twice your annual income.

Meaning, if you make $60,000 per year, you could afford a house roughly around $120,000. However, with mortgage rates hovering around 5 percent, at the time of this writing, your affordability factor jumps up three to four times your annual income. In other words, the first-time home you could afford is possibly somewhere around the $180,000 to $240,000 mark.

Use the table below to help you determine how much house you can afford to buy at the current interest rate level.

TABLE: HOW MUCH HOUSE CAN YOU AFFORD?

1. Your Gross Monthly Income: _____

2. Multiply by one of the following
percentages: x _____
 .25 (25%), conservative for lender and
   you
 .28 (28%), still somewhat conservative
 .33 (33%), to allow you some debt
   payments too
 .36 (36%), to allow more with debt
   payments

3. Calculate and then subtract your total
current monthly debt to service:
 Credit cards   _____
 Car loan / Lease   + _____
 Charge accounts   + _____
 School loans   + _____
 Other personal debt   + _____
 Total debt to service   _____

4. Maximum available for monthly
   mortgage payment: _____

5. Multiply by 12 (months of year): x _____

6. Annual mortgage payment: _____

7. Divide by current rate of interest (___%): / _____

8. Total amount available for mortgage: _____

9. Plus cash available for the down
   payment: + _____

10. Approximate amount you can spend
    for a home: _____

What is so cool about this exercise is that it gives you not only a sense of what you could feasibly tackle financially when it comes to making a monthly mortgage payment, it also accurately illustrates that how much house you can afford changes depending on which interest rate you apply.

For example, in the table above, if you got to line #4 and figured out that you could roughly afford $2,000 in a monthly mortgage payment, then took that $2,000 and multiplied it by 12 in line #5, you figured out that your annual affordable mortgage payment (on line #6) would be $24,000. Here is the breakdown of what line #8 would look like with a few different interest rates in our current economic ballpark and a bit higher.

Annual Mortgage Payment	Interest Rate	Total Mortgage Amount
$24,000	5%	$480,000
$24,000	6%	$400,000
$24,000	6.5%	$369,230
$24,000	7%	$342,857

As you can easily see, the difference is dramatic. A 5 percent interest rate vs. a 7 percent interest rate increases the size of your affordability factor by a whopping 33 percent!

I have listed another table on page 30 for you to play around with to give you even more perspective on your mortgage payments vs. the amount you want to borrow—the loan's interest rate—and the length of years your mortgage payment will last. This table will be helpful when it comes to shopping for lenders, which we will discuss more at length in chapter 4. To determine the monthly payment for your mortgage, you will need to first find the rate of interest you would hypothetically be paying from the first column of the table and then you would scroll across to the right to find the correct number that correlates with a fifteen-year or a thirty-year loan. Meaning, if you are looking to get into a $200,000 mortgage loan situation and you secure a 5.5 percent loan for 30 years, you would find 5.5 percent in the left column and scroll to the right under the 30 year column to find the number 5.68. You would then take the loan amount of $200,000 and drop the last three digits of zeros to come up with a calculation that looks like this:

200 × 5.68 = $1136.00 Monthly Mortgage Payment

MONTHLY MORTGAGE PAYMENT CALCULATOR

Interest Rate	15-Year Mortgage	30-Year Mortgage
4.00%	7.40	4.77
4.50%	7.65	5.07
5.00%	7.91	5.37
5.25%	8.04	5.53
5.50%	8.17	5.68
5.75%	8.31	5.84
6.00%	8.44	6.00
6.25%	8.58	6.16
6.50%	8.71	6.32
6.75%	8.85	6.49
7.00%	8.99	6.65
7.25%	9.13	6.83
7.50%	9.27	6.99
7.75%	9.42	7.17
8.00%	9.56	7.34

PITI

When you start to get into the world of real estate, one of the first things you'll notice is that it has a language, slang, and jargon all its own. A term you'll run into a lot is PITI, an acronym we discussed at the beginning of the chapter that means, essentially, your monthly mortgage payment. PITI stands for **P**rincipal, **I**nterest, **T**axes, and **I**nsurance, or the four components of your mortgage payment. Understanding how all four parts work together will ultimately allow you to tally up the different costs and really figure out what you can afford for your first home.

PITI = Principal, Interest, Taxes, Insurance

Principal & Interest . . . of the PITI

Your mortgage payments of principal and interest are paid monthly and are exactly what they sound like: The *principal* is the amount you borrowed to buy your property, and the *interest* is the money that the bank charges you for that. In the early years of a mortgage, the majority of your monthly mortgage payment will be going to service the interest on the loan, not the principal. As your mortgage matures, less of the monthly payment will be going toward the interest payment, and more will be going toward the principal loan amount. That is why there is such a heavy focus on the interest rate you are able to secure on your loan, what type of mortgage you choose, and how long you plan to realistically stay in your first home!

Here's an example: Grace found a great condo with a purchase price of $150,000. She had a down payment of just $10,000, which meant that she needed to get a $140,000 mortgage. Her mortgage, a thirty-year fixed-rate at 6 percent, was a good deal. But after thirty years, Grace will have paid back the $140,000 in principal *and* a whopping $200,892 bucks in interest . . . much of it in the early years of her loan. The good news: As we discussed earlier, the interest is tax deductible. Hence, Grace will be able to deduct $200,892 over thirty years on her gross income during that time period.

Taxes . . . of the PITI

Real estate tax generally runs about 1.5 percent of the purchase of the property value (but it varies by region) and is generally billed in one big chunk once a year. You will want to understand what the exact tax rate is in your area by calling the tax collector's office in the town where you are contemplating buying a home. You will also want to ask not only what the property tax is, but also what additional fees and assessments may apply.

If you put down less than 20 percent of the purchase of your first home, the lender will require you to create a tax escrow account with them, on your behalf, in addition to your mortgage. The real estate tax will be put in the escrow account, which is in effect a non-interest-bearing savings account. This account assures the lender that the loan's collateral will not be sold or seized for nonpayment of property taxes. This means that if your real estate semi-annual or annual tax bill will be broken down into monthly payments, then that will be included in your monthly mortgage payment.

Insurance . . . of the PITI

As with real estate taxes, if you put down less than 20 percent of the loan value, lenders will require you to purchase homeowners insurance, also known as private mortgage insurance (PMI), and create an insurance escrow on your behalf so that the property will not be lost to fire or other catastrophe—or the simple fact that if you have very little financial stake in the deal up front, you could, in effect, just walk away and skip to Europe to play for a year if you changed your mind!

You should buy the most comprehensive insurance with the highest deductible, that you can afford, to minimize the cost. The premium price depends mainly upon the purchase price of the home, the type of mortgage you have selected, and, of course, which policy you sign up for. You can expect to pay anywhere from $50 and up per month for every $100,000 of the loan amount. Don't worry—you don't have to come up with the full amount at the closing. It's a one-time payment, borrowed at the closing, and then repaid monthly or annually. The good news is that the interest is tax deductible too! A last piece of good news on the PMI front is that after you are in your home for a few years and your equity reaches a certain percentage—usually 20 percent—you are allowed to cancel you PMI policy.

It is important to realize that it is your responsibility to bring up cancellation with your lender when you qualify for it—they won't necessarily remind you! A good many homebuyers are not aware of this and pay unnecessary PMI long after they technically need it. And, per the Homeowner's Protection Act of 1998, your lender is required to cancel your PMI when you reach 22 percent equity . . . whether you request it or not. Remember, canceling your PMI as soon as possible can save you thousands over the life of your loan.

The most important part of budgeting for a home is being realistic about what is truly affordable for you at this time. Remember, your dream home may actually be three house purchases away. For most of us single women, purchasing our first home will be about the opportunity to build some home equity and get our feet wet learning how this entire process works, so that we are no longer novices at home buying. The first time around may not be about the ideal neighborhood, size, or amenities. Be prudent and patient with yourself when it comes to what you can really afford to buy, so that your first home experience is a positive, happy one!

3

Is My Credit Good Enough?

The Truth About Credit Reports, and How to Make Your Finances Mortgage-Ready

Don't fear mistakes. There are none!
—Miles Davis

Erica knows it's a great time to buy. But there's one major thing stopping her: her credit history.

It's not exactly that she has terrible credit. There was the student loan that she missed a few payments on, and a couple of late credit-card payments back when she was laid off two years ago. She's back on her feet now, with a good job that's stable and pretty lucrative. She makes her payments on time, but she does have several thousand dollars on a couple of different credit cards.

The fact is, Erica doesn't really know what her credit score is, or what it needs to be to make her a good candidate for home ownership. And she's kind of afraid of what she'll find out if she starts to investigate.

* * *

One of the first things any prospective homebuyer has to start preparing for is the fact that you're going to be divulging a lot of very personal financial information about yourself to a whole plethora of people. Your money life may, in some cases, become the proverbial "open book." Your bank account and credit history will be given an in-depth examination—how much you have in savings, checking, debt, and credit are all fair game. And the fact is, as a single person (especially a single woman) buying solo, you may face some skepticism about whether your pocketbook is up for the challenge. The key, then, is to make your finances as impeccable as possible . . . and that means, first and foremost, improving or repairing your credit.

As we just discussed, there are many affordable mortgages out there, no matter what your monthly budget may look like today. Some mortgages may even cover the entire purchase price of your first home. What all these low- or no-money-down mortgages have in common is that they are heavily dependent on what type of credit you have.

So, what if you don't have great credit? What if you are carrying high credit-card balances? What if you have a few late payments or have even defaulted on a loan? What about a bankruptcy? And, the worst-case scenario, you've had a foreclosure? Can you still get a lender to extend you an affordable loan? In this chapter, we'll discuss how credit problems can affect your ability to get real estate financing. We'll also talk about some creative ways to address some of the obstacles you may encounter, if you are credit challenged, to help you secure a mortgage for your first home purchase.

Getting FICO Fit

When you apply for a mortgage, you will be asked to fill out a standard questionnaire with about fifty questions that cover your personal finances, including: your income, your expenses, the amount of money you plan to put down, your money in the bank, your long-term debt, and much more. The lender will then take a look at your FICO scores.

What is FICO? It is the most popular credit scoring system used by lenders to help streamline the credit application processing system. FICO is actually an abbreviation for the company that developed this system—Fair Isaac COorporation (www.fairissac.com). FICO scores can vary from the 300s to the 900s, with most scores ending up in the 600s to 700s. The higher your score, the more likely that you will be able to make timely and complete payments when borrowing money . . . and the better chance you'll have of getting a good mortgage rate. A very respectable score is in the 680–700 range. At these levels, you will most likely be able to find a good deal on a mortgage. Remember, the lower your score, the more you will have to pay in interest and possibly down payment to actually secure real estate financing. So getting FICO fit is a priority when it comes to buying your first home. Take a look at the following chart, it indicates the odds for satisfactory repayment of your credit obligation:

FICO Score	Odds of Good Payers to Bad Payer*
Below 600	8 to 1
620–659	26 to 1
660–679	38 to 1
680–699	55 to 1
700–719	123 to 1
720–759	323 to 1
760–799	597 to 1
Above 800	1292 to 1

*A bad payer is a 90+ days late.

Three major reporting agencies (Equifax, Experian, TransUnion) individually review your credit report and then give you a score. Lenders will generally take all three companies' scores into consideration when reviewing your FICO score. If you have a 680 from Equifax, a 620 from Experian, and a 660 from TransUnion, then you can count on your score being viewed as an approximate 650.

There are several key elements that affect your credit score on an ongoing basis (meaning every thirty days)—here is the breakdown that you should be aware of.

Payment History = 35 Percent of Your FICO Score

What is your track record with repaying prior loans? A lender wants to see that you have had a perfect payment record with timely repayment of borrowed money. Late payments reduce your credit score. In fact, recent late payments are more indicative of future default than those that occurred more than twenty-four months ago. A thirty-day late payment within the last thirty days will reduce your credit score more than a bankruptcy filed five years ago with clean credit since. No kidding! Think of your credit score as a moving snapshot of your financial health based mainly on current events rather than ones that occurred years ago. Needless to say, timely payments increase your credit score. The fewer lates, judgments, liens, or collections the better. Zero "derogs" (derogatory notations) on your credit report usually indicate lower risk to a lender.

The Amount You Owe on Current Debt = 30 Percent

The more you owe, the lower your score. Think of it this way, the closer you are to maxxing out your current lines of credit (i.e., credit cards or direct loans), the more your score will be affected negatively. It is suggested that low balances on several credit cards is better than high balances on a few cards. And, if possible, your balances should be kept to at least 30 percent or less of your potential credit line availability. Lenders have learned through time that statistically they are less likely to be repaid by borrowers with big existing debts. That is why it is strongly recommended that you don't buy a brand-new car if you are thinking of buying a house!

One last thing to remember: Too many credit cards can be detrimental, but only if the first or second reason code states too many credit cards on your credit report. Meaning, when your credit report is actually run, the credit agencies will tell you on your report if you have too many credit cards given your financial profile. You will want to look for this, if you think this may be you! In truth, there is a healthy financial balance that lenders look for regarding the number of lines of credit you have available. You want to keep as many of your credit card accounts open as is necessary to illustrate to lenders that you have a balanced credit history of paying your debts off in a timely, reasonable manner. Yet, if you have thirty credit cards that add up to $150,000 in lines of unsecured credit, then you may make a lender nervous about offering you a home loan for the same amount—even if you have a total of only $5,000 of outstanding credit card debt on those thirty cards. Who knows . . . with all that available credit you might have the temptation to "go crazy" with your plastic, and that could potentially be a problem for your bank when it comes to you repaying your loan. Hence, you want to keep the older credit lines around for history and credibility; but you do not want to have too much credit availability either.

TIP:

Review your credit report with a mortgage broker or savvy real estate agent who can help analyze your credit profile to best advise you before you close any credit card accounts. Remember, closing these accounts could end up being the worst possible thing for your profile and your credit score could go down. Make a point to ask for help if you are concerned about this scenario for yourself.

The Length of Your Credit History = 15 Percent

A lender prefers to see a long track record of success when it comes to your use of credit, as it indicates lower risk. The longer your credit history, the greater the probability you will receive a higher credit score. Your credit report will detail when each of your credit accounts and loans began. Opening lots of new accounts and closing seasoned accounts will have a negative impact on your credit score. Many of us have developed a habit of "credit surfing"—jumping from one credit card to the next to take advantage of the next low interest rate or cash-back program. While that's not always a bad thing, it's important to have a mix of older credit accounts and newer ones, too.

So what to do if you don't have a long and venerable credit history established yet? Generally speaking, a brief credit history does not automatically indicate a higher credit risk. Applicants with limited credit history can still score high on their FICO scores, as long as you're not a "heavy user" of credit and your payments have been paid on time. The credit reporting agencies look for at least two credit accounts in good standing that have been open for at least six months.

New Credit = 10 Percent

It is a general assumption that when people begin to struggle financially, they tend to seek out new loans to keep afloat. If you have opened five new lines of credit in the last six months, that will be a red flag to the credit-reporting agencies. But in this instance, the type of credit line you've established will matter as much as the quantity. Finance company lines of credit will score lower than a line of credit from a bank or a department store. For example, if you have opened up new credit card accounts, you will be raising more red flags that will lower your credit score, due to the nature of how credit cards work and the detriment they can cause to your overall financial health with high interest rates and over abuse. Whereas a bank or department store credit line is considered less detrimental, as banks don't tend to make outrageous offers with high interest rates and what department stores offer by way of credit lines tends to be limited as well.

Financial Healthiness of Credit in Current Use = 10 Percent

Lenders consider too much high-interest consumer debt (credit cards) or not enough borrowing to buy investments, such as real estate (which appreciates in value), a negative for financial health. Meaning, if you have lots of credit card debt, but no real assets, such as CDs, bonds, stocks, or real estate purchases within your credit report, then you will be considered less financially sound.

What WON'T Affect My Credit Rating?

There are a number of myths about what type of credit report inquiries do and do not affect your credit rating negatively. I have broken the list down for you to demystify what you may or may not have heard. Will the following situations affect your credit rating?

- **Applying for a new credit card just before a credit check.** Is this a credit risk? Maybe not. But if the credit bureau sees you applying for several new credit cards in a short period of time *and* your other existing accounts are "maxxed out" this can send a bad sign.

- **Applying for a mortgage with multiple lenders in a short period of time.** Despite what unscrupulous lenders might tell you, multiple credit inquiries, regardless of the number, for mortgages or autos within a fourteen-day period of time are only counted as one inquiry. Any mortgage or auto inquiry made about an applicant's credit file within thirty days of the lender's inquiry will be shown on the credit report, but will not adversely impact the applicant's credit score.

- **An employer's credit check.** Promotional or employer inquiries do not adversely impact an applicant's score. Only inquiries authorized by the applicant for the granting of credit can impact an applicant's score.

In summary, your credit information about past payment performance, credit utilization, and credit history will carry the most weight in a credit score. Credit scores automatically improve as your overall credit picture improves. Which is great news for those of us who aren't feeling so hot about how we may be looking in the credit-scoring arena. It is important to understand how the system works so you can make yourself credit-worthy *before* buying a first home. The important thing to remember is this: No matter what your financial snapshot looks like today, you *can* repair your credit and find a loan.

Fannie Mae and Freddie Mac Have the Power!

The way the entire home-financing process works today is different than one would expect. In fact, the company whose name appears on your mortgage documents is just the company that services the loan, but not the company that actually comes up with the funds to make your mortgage happen. There is a good percentage chance that the money comes from one of two quasi-government corporations that lend billions of dollars on real estate, known as secondary lenders: Fannie Mae and Freddie Mac.

The system works like this: You apply for a loan from mortgage broker "Hal." Hal sends your application to a mortgage company, which in turn forwards your application to the underwriting department of Fannie Mae or Freddie Mac. The underwriters will then look at your mortgage application and FICO score and apply a profile of their own. Once their evaluation is complete, Fannie Mae will report back to the mortgage company to let them know what loan you will get and for how much. In effect, the mortgage company tells Hal, and Hal then tells you.

Fannie Mae and Freddie Mac have an enormous database of successful and unsuccessful profiles that your application will be measured against. From their database they create profiles of what successful applicants look like and then see how yours fits in. They'll then establish a "grade" based on your profile. You will end up with a letter grade anywhere from *A* to *D*.

There are some borrowers that lenders are absolutely sure will repay. These are the "prime" borrowers. These folk have no credit problems, strong incomes, and lots of cash in the bank. They are known as the *A* borrowers.

Everyone else, well, they are all called "sub-prime" (*A-* down to *D*) borrowers, whom the lender on some level is concerned will not repay their loan. Take a look at the chart below, it is a general overview of the grading system that underwriters use:

YOUR CREDIT RATING EXPLAINED

A	You are a creditworthy Goddess!
A-	One unpaid bill, no more than $1,000 bucks, turned into collection or no more than one late payment of over sixty days or two late payments of over thirty days in credit cards or installment debt within the past two years. No bankruptcies or foreclosures on record (for at least the previous seven years).
B	Within the past one and a half years, you have up to four late payments of no more than thirty days for credit cards or installment debt. You may have had bankruptcy or a foreclosure concluded at least two years before applying for loan.

C Within the past year, you have racked up as many as six late payments of no more than thirty days on credit cards or installment debt. You may have accounts currently in collection, but the mortgage may be granted if they are no more than $5,000 in total and paid in full by the time the mortgage is funded. Mortgage funds may be used to clean up these debts. If you have a bankruptcy, it was resolved a year before applying for mortgage. If you had a foreclosure, it was concluded at least two years before applying for the loan.

D You have many current late payments, have several accounts in collection, and have judgments against you. These can be paid off from the proceeds of the new mortgage. If you have a bankruptcy, it was concluded more than six months before you applied for the new mortgage. If you had a foreclosure, it was concluded at least two years before applying for the loan.

Today, if you are *severely* sub-prime, as indicated on the chart above, you still have the ability to find creative ways to buy your first home. We'll discuss those options in greater detail in the chapter 5, so keep reading. Keep a bigger picture perspective on this credit conundrum, too; the preceding credit-rating explanation is really just a general reference point to allow you to get a sense of how the system works. The more you know how the system works, the more you will be able to utilize the system working for you! Exceptions to rules are always made, especially when the monetary supply is flowing and mortgage lenders are competing to get your business as a first-time homebuyer.

Why Is Your Credit Messed Up?

Poor Choice in Friends
You co-signed on a loan for a friend who defaulted. You kindly offered your good credit to help a college buddy secure a car loan and they ran off with the car and stuck you with the payments. Most likely, you refused making payments for the five years on something you don't own or couldn't even sell. Good that you don't want the debt, but bad for creditors who see that you "took a hike" when things got tough!

No Job, Poor Health, Divorce, Death in the Family
These excuses will be most helpful if you actually have a long track record of good credit, followed by a short period of bad credit (approximately six months), and then good credit again (at minimum two years)—as it shows why you had late payments and that it was for a particular reason over a short period of time.

You Bit Off More Than You Could Chew
This one could be a foreclosure issue. Let's say you got swept up in the dot.com mania and bought before the market tanked. You could no longer afford the mortgage and had to move back East to find a decent paying job. You failed to keep up the property and lost it to foreclosure. However, that was a few years ago, your situation is different now, and you have definitely learned your lesson.

Remember, the very best way to approach lenders is to be absolutely up front about the issues at hand. If you wait till they find the problem or till it surfaces, it just looks even worse. Have a letter ready that provides them with a very clear explanation of why you had late payments, defaulted on a loan, or even were foreclosed upon. It is important to note in each situation why circumstances are different now! Besides, even if you don't end up finding a deal with a fully assumable no-qualifying FHA (Federal Housing Association) mortgage, you can always use this file of credit history explanations that you create to your advantage when seeking to secure another type of financing from a lender. This is an incredibly useful exercise. If you have a checkered credit history, take the time to create this file for yourself—it could not only make the difference when achieving financing, but it could also save you a lot of money over the long haul in the interest rate you end up paying on your mortgage!

I have missed more than nine thousand shots in my career. I have lost almost three hundred games. On twenty-six occasions I have been entrusted to take the game-winning shot . . . and missed. I have failed over and over again in my life. And that is why I succeed.
—*Michael Jordan*

Can My Credit Be Improved?

Yes. Your credit has the ability to repair itself over time. Remember, your credit is an ongoing snapshot of your financial picture, which changes each month to reflect your most recent activities. By simply paying all your bills on time, making a plan to pay off your current debts, and building cash reserves—you will be improving your credit.

What If My Credit Report Has an Error?

Good question. Federal laws require that credit-reporting agencies delete any information that is inaccurate, erroneous, or obsolete when it is brought to their attention. You should contact the credit bureau in writing, and according to the Federal Trade Commission, a credit bureau must respond to your correspondence within thirty days. But this is often a lot easier said than done.

Most experts agree that, in order to get an erroneous credit listing off your credit report, it's best to go to the source of the error. Remember, credit bureaus just report the information that's given to them. If, for example, your report shows an unpaid bill to a particular credit card company (and you've never had an account with that company), give the credit card company a call directly to straighten this out. It can take some time for the correction to work its way into your report, so the process of checking your credit is best done *before* you make an offer on your dream home. Otherwise, those discrepancies can put a monkey wrench into the process.

There are many credit-repair companies that can help you address your credit issues for a set fee. Their fees are not small, but given the difficulties in correcting these problems and the time that it may take you to do so, it may be worth it.

The most challenging part of this equation is obtaining the proof. What is normally acceptable to the credit agencies is a letter or document, from the lender that reported the bad credit, saying it was a mistake. Or a mistaken identity may be corrected by showing proof in the form of a birth certificate, driver's license, etc.

Keep in mind that there is a two-step process to correcting bad credit. You must first write a letter explaining the problem and why it is definitely the creditor's fault or an error of the credit-reporting bureau. Second, you need to submit the documentation to back up your argument.

How Long Does It Take to Have an Error Corrected?

Well, it all depends on the proof that you have. If you have a letter or documentation from the original creditor who reported an error, the credit bureau will normally remove the offending report in thirty days.

However, if it becomes a "he said" vs. a "she said" situation, it is an entirely different process. As a rule, credit-reporting agencies are required to insert your letters of explanation within your report, along with the bad report, and may make them available to those who ask for the reports.

Keep in mind: The credit agency does not take sides. In a disputed incident, the error will most likely not be removed and you can plan on it staying on your report for the usual seven years.

Again, this is why working with a credit repair company, may be hugely beneficial to you at the end of the day.

You may also contact the Federal Trade Commission for more information on how to correct an error on your credit report:

Federal Trade Commission
600 Pennsylvania Avenue, N W
Washington, DC 20580
1-877-FTC-HELP (382-4357)
www.ftc.gov/

In a nutshell, mistakes and errors can be fixed. Other problems may not be fixable.

Credit problems that can be fixed:

- The wrong name or address is on the report.

- Someone else's social security number is on your report.

- A creditor made a mistake in reporting a late payment.

- A creditor has not removed a loan that's in your name, even though it's been paid off.

- You redeemed your property, yet it shows up as a foreclosure.

- You did not file for bankruptcy, yet one shows up against you.

Challenging credit issues that most likely cannot be fixed . . . except over time:

- Late payments (without reason).

- Missed payment (without reason).

- Loan defaults.

- Bankruptcies.

- Foreclosures.

Get a Copy of Your Credit Report

Experts suggest that you review a copy of your credit report at least once a year. It is estimated that one out of every three credit reports has errors listed within it. You will definitely want to review your credit report before applying for a mortgage to strategize your position. Plus, you are allowed to obtain at least one copy of your credit report each year with no penalty to you, and the cost is minimal.

TransUnion
800-888-4213
www.tuc.com

Experian
800-493-2392
www.experian.com

Equifax
800-685-1111
www.equifax.com

What About No Credit History?

Having no credit technically could be considered equal to having bad credit. With no credit, lenders have no way to establish your money-management skills or your ability to repay a loan. The good news is that it is not a doomed situation and, with a little bit of persistence and the proper efforts, you have the possibility to start a good credit record and be years ahead of the individual who begins with lots of bad reports.

The process of creating a paper trail to establish good credit history that is identifiable to a lender may take you six to twelve months before applying for a mortgage. Following is a simple-step process to help you get started:

Go to your bank and request a debit card from your checking or savings account. This card, which is based only on your assets in the bank, acts just like a credit card.

You will want to use your debit card as frequently as possible to illustrate that you can manage your money successfully. Don't bounce checks, and always cover any checks from others that you deposit. See if your bank will offer you overdraft protection, just in case you run short. Banks usually do for their good customers.

Once you have your debit card and overdraft protection, you will want to ask your bank for a credit card.

Once you get your credit card, use it frequently and repay it promptly and completely each month. You'll begin to establish a credit history after just three months of using your credit card.

Shortly thereafter, you should begin receiving other great credit card offers. Apply for two others with the most competitive rates and no annual fees. Once you receive them, charge up to 30 percent or less of the credit line and then make regular monthly payments.

Now, go back to your bank and ask for a non-collateral loan—a line of credit. Since you have history at your bank, your new credit cards, plus no bad credit—this should be a no-brainer. Plan to borrow a thousand dollars, make regular payments, and, after a few months, pay it back.

Not taking into consideration longevity, you have just established prime credit!

If you don't have time to wait six months to a year, it may still be possible to establish credit for yourself to make it happen with a lender for a mortgage. In some form or another, you have credit history; you just need to be thorough in checking what you have as proof to fill it with. Here are a few suggestions:

Rent and Utility Receipts

One of the easiest ways to show a steady pattern of payments is through your basic monthly expenses. If you paid for these bills by checks, gather those canceled checks. You may also request a letter from your landlord or the utility companies confirming that you made your payments on time. You will want to ask the landlord to include the rent amount paid each month to illustrate that you can handle a large monthly payment.

Informal Loans

Gather canceled checks from payback of loans from friends or family. You will also want to get the person to sign a statement/letter (with a corporate or business name, if possible) showing the amount borrowed, term, when the payback payments were made, and when the full amount was finalized.

You will want to take a little time to explore other possibilities of payment history, which could help you illustrate a healthy financial snapshot of yourself to a lender. Although this type of credit history is not ideal for a lender, it can go a long way in helping make your first home purchase a reality!

Consumer Debt, or the Power of Plastic

Another important issue facing many young women today is consumer debt, otherwise known as credit card debt. You are not alone. I know how prevalent credit card debt is for young women. We're enticed with credit card offers from the time we're old enough to drive, and sometimes it seems like "everybody's doing it"—charging the latest shoes, music, or meal rather than staying within a strict budget.

But the truth is (and I know you already know this) . . . consumer debt is truly horrific, and it can really hinder your chances to get ahead financially. Unlike the interest on a mortgage loan payment, the interest you pay on your credit card debt is not tax deductible. Consumer debt severely affects your ability to afford a mortgage and, in some cases, even qualify for one. Some experts say that consumer debt is the equivalent of having financial cancer!

If you are currently in debt, take a look at my first book, *Get in the Game!: The Girls' Guide to Money & Investing*. I dedicated almost an entire chapter to exploring a number of commonsense ways to tackle debt. For now, here are a few tips to consider when it comes to getting a handle on your credit card debt. If you have more than one piece of cold hard plastic, gather up all the bills you can find. Now, I want you to casually glance at all of your outstanding balances and begin to make a list, like the sleek sample list below, of these balances. Add to the list the annual percentage rate you are currently offered on each card.

Creditor	Balance Owed	Interest Rate
Clothing store	$1,500	20%
MasterCard	$1,750	15%
Dad	$500	0%
Visa	$2,100	8.9%

Feel like you're bonding with your debt? Congratulate yourself for exposing the truth about you and your credit card habits. You have two options available to you. If you have bad credit, you will want to make a plan to pay off the credit cards with the highest rate of interest first and make minimum payments on the other credit card balances. Once that highest rate of interest credit card is paid off, you will want to move on with this system to the credit card with the next highest rate of interest and so on.

If you have good credit, you will want to consolidate all your credit card debt onto the one card with the lowest annual percentage rate. If you do not have a credit card that is offering you a low annual percentage rate (low in today's meaty credit card marketplace is something like 5.0 percent), then apply for one that offers you such a rate. Keep in mind that credit card companies vie for your financial affairs, and if you have a pleasant credit history, then they should make it very easy for you to slip into another credit card situation they are offering.

If you decide to shop around for a lower-rate card, check out the website www.cardweb.com, or call 301-631-9100. This site offers a ton of detailed information on different credit cards, rates, fees, and perks such as frequent flyer awards. Lastly, don't forget to check back from time to time on your credit report, as it will be improving as you begin to pay off your debt on each credit card. This may, in fact, eventually qualify you for a lower-rate card to transfer your remaining credit card balances onto!

You're probably getting the gist of this: Consumer debt and mortgages don't mix well. Make a plan to pay off as much of your debt as possible and do the best you can to make sure your credit is as sterling as possible. Your chance of getting a great deal on a first-time home is greatly affected by your credit history. The better your credit and the less consumer debt you carry, the better rates and terms you will be offered for your mortgage.

If tackling your credit is nerve-wracking, you are not alone! Most everyone I speak with—not just young single women—get pretty jittery when it comes to pulling their credit report. Just pull it anyway . . . and address whatever may need to be addressed!

If you are feeling overwhelmed by all of this new information, keep in mind that *most* people have specific challenges with their credit history in one form or another. This process isn't about beating yourself up; this is about getting the facts and finding a way to make them work for you when it comes to gaining access to buying your first home. Even if you feel you are not totally ready to shop for a first home today, apply for a copy of your credit report and make a plan to review it thoroughly with a mortgage lender. Empower yourself with the facts today so that you may plan for your mortgage loan tomorrow.

4

What Kind of
Mortgage Should
I Get?

Fixed Rate, Adjustable Rate, "Points,"
and All the Other Lingo You Need to Know

You must take your chance
—William Shakespeare

Gabrielle has been dutifully doing her home-buying homework—the past two months she's been scouring the websites and newspapers around the Atlanta area, where she lives and works as a teacher, looking at possible neighborhoods and properties. She's also started looking into a mortgage, even going so far as to apply for a mortgage online. Gabby has a good financial record, and she's been bombarded with letters and e-mails from lenders and mortgage brokers who are hungry for her business.

But all the jargon has really started to overwhelm her. The rates they're offering her run the gamut: thirty-year, 5.5 percent fixed rate? An adjustable-rate loan, with a 5.625 per-

cent rate fixed for the first five years? No points? One point? How in the heck is she supposed to know what's best for her?

* * *

Now that we've addressed that big question—"How Much House Can I Afford?"—in chapter 2, and you've found out how creditworthy you are in chapter 3, it's time to start investigating how you'll actually pay for your dream house. It's time to start shopping for your mortgage.

The good news: There is a wealth of choices when it comes to mortgages. The bad news: There is a wealth of choices. It can get confusing, especially if this is your first time negotiating the real estate labyrinth. I will forewarn you now: This chapter is the meatiest one of the book. But understanding this information is crucial to getting the best deal on your home—making it both a great place to live *and* a great investment in your future.

Time to Go Shopping!

For many of us, the notion of "shopping" for a mortgage is a tough one to get our minds around. Shouldn't we just go begging, hat in hand, to our local bank and be grateful that somebody, *anybody*, will give us a loan that we'll spend the next thirty years paying off? Actually, no. Just like you scour the Web and newspapers for the best bargains on a cute pair of boots or a new car, there are definitely "deals" to be had when shopping for a mortgage. You don't want to have to spend more than what you must. You will want to find the most affordable mortgage for you right now, with today's economic climate and interest-rate conditions, which will allow you to get into that first home ASAP at the cheapest rates that work best for your overall financial situation. In order for you to get outfitted for the best mortgage that meets your specific financial requirements, you will need to understand the options available to you when it comes to mastering a mortgage.

To Fix or to Adjust?

This could be a tagline for that new pair of leather pants that "almost" fits you perfectly! But we're not talking about hemming a pair of trousers . . . in real estate parlance, fixed-rate vs. adjustable-rate is the big difference in all the different types of mortgages available to you. In essence, you will have the option to choose a fixed-rate mortgage, an adjustable-rate mortgage, or a mix of the two—which is referred to as a hybrid loan.

Fix It and Forget It

As indicated by its name, a *fixed-rate loan* has interest rates that are fixed over the life of the loan—usually, a fifteen- or thirty-year period. As you may have guessed, with a fixed-rate mortgage, your monthly payments stay the same because the rate of interest that you are charged on your mortgage (loan) stays the same. This type of mortgage is incredibly attractive during times of low interest-rate environments, like the one we are in at the time of this writing. I have had friends who luckily locked into a fixed-rate mortgage for a meager 4 percent in late 2003, which is amazing! Especially when you consider the fact that just two years earlier rates hovered around 8 percent, and four years earlier they were around 10 to 11 percent. In order to give you a sense of what a big deal a little fluctuation in the rate of interest makes on your monthly mortgage payment, let's take a look at the following examples:

Interest Rate Charged on $100,000 Loan	Regular Monthly Payment
5%	$416.67
6%	$500.00
7%	$583.33
8%	$666.67

As you can see, the difference between a 5 percent rate and an 8 percent rate ends up meaning a whole heck of a lot more dough each month that you will need to cough up. In essence, this could be the difference between you affording to buy that first home, or not! Another important factor to note: Fixed-rate mortgages are less risky. You won't have to live with the uncertainty of wondering where interest rates are going and whether you will be able to afford your new monthly mortgage payment should interest rates rise.

Adjustable Rates

As for an adjustable-rate mortgage (ARM is the abbreviated real estate–jargon term), as mentioned earlier, your interest rate fluctuates according to the market. The rate a borrower is charged is usually tied to an economic index (like the stock market or Treasury bills), and is periodically adjusted up or down according to the market's performance. There are three main types of ARMs: one-year ARMs (adjust every year), three-year ARMs (adjust every three years), and five-year ARMs (adjust every five years). The relationship is pretty simple: If interest rates are on the rise, the likelihood is that your ARM rate of interest on your mortgage will rise, which means your monthly mortgage payment amount will most likely increase too! The good news is that when interest rates begin to fall overall, your ARM and mortgage payment will probably fall too.

So, why would someone opt for the riskiness of an adjustable-rate loan rather than the relatively sure bet of a fixed rate? Well, for one thing the starting rate on an ARM is generally very low—lower than on a fixed-rate loan. If you're sure that you'll only be in your home for a short period of time, or you want to gamble that interests rates will continue to go down rather than creep upward, an ARM might be the right choice for you.

Hybrid Loans

So, fixed-rate mortgage vs. ARM is the basic breakdown of your options . . . but of course, it's not quite that easy. There's another type of loan you'll run into—a hybrid loan, which is a combination of fixed-rate and adjustable-rate loans. In many cases, these loans begin as fixed-rate loans, most likely for a period of three, five, or seven years. After that it will transition into either a fixed-rate loan at the current market percentage (called a *convertible loan*), or it will transition into an adjustable-rate loan that fluctuates every year (called a *nonconvertible loan*).

Hybrid loans can be extremely attractive to first-time homebuyers whose number-one priority will most certainly be the A factor—AFFORDABILITY. They're also great for single women who aren't sure whether they want to commit to a home for the life of a full thirty-year mortgage! We are looking to lock in to the lowest mortgage rate available to us—to make our first-time home purchase happen. In particular, these two-step mortgages or hybrid loans could be a full percentage point (or more) below the rate on a thirty-year fixed-rate mortgage. Why? It is called the *risk reward factor*, which is considered in all financial deals. If a lender offers you a deal in which you are guaranteed a fixed rate over a thirty-year period, they are taking on more risk, because that is a huge chunk of time in which no one really knows what direction interest rates will move or what will truly happen over that period, economically speaking. If you lock in to a 6 percent fixed-rate mortgage over a thirty-year period and interest rates skyrocket to 10 percent in ten years, the lender is left holding the bag.

Ever talk to folks (like my parents) who bought homes back in the late 1970s or early 1980s? If they were like my mom, they probably had to face interest rates in the neighborhood of 18 to 20 percent—numbers that seem positively shocking today. What this all boils down to for you is that a lender who guarantees you a fixed rate, especially in today's low-interest rate, slower economic cycle, is going to charge you more interest compared to what you could get with an ARM, two-step mortgage, or some other type of hybrid loan.

For many of us looking to buy our first place, even a small difference in interest rates can make a big difference in whether we can afford to buy today or not. Your first home is probably going to be what most people refer to as a *starter home.* It is a way to stop paying rent, begin tackling and taking control of your finances, and for heavens' sake, build some bountiful Oprah-like home equity for yourself. It is completely reasonable to think that your dream home won't happen for another three or even four houses down the road. This book is geared specifically to help you make getting into your first home a reality. Having said that, a two-step mortgage or even some type of other hybrid loan, which we will discuss later, allows you to lock in a lower rate of interest initially (a *teaser rate* in real estate jargon) than a fixed-rate loan. Then the rate may increase after a few years. There are some risks involved in ARMs and hybrid mortgages, but they're definitely worth considering and a great way to make a deal happen.

If you truly can't stomach the risk associated with the unknowns of fluctuating interest rates either in the immediate-term or the longer-term picture—and perhaps you may even see yourself in your home for that very long fifteen- or thirty-year mortgage scenario—by all means, do find yourself the best deal possible on a fixed-rate loan!

Where to Find Information About Mortgages

- **Real Estate Agents and Brokers.** Your real estate agent's firm probably owns a mortgage company. Ask her for several recommendations, including a few companies not owned by her firm.
- **Local Banks.** Visit your local lending institution and ask for information about mortgages.
- **Newspapers.** The real estate section of your newspaper isn't just a place to find property listings; you'll also find ads from local mortgage companies along with their current loans and rates. These rates change almost daily, so when you call don't simply ask for the price you saw listed in the ad. Ask them what their best price is on the loan you're interested in.
- **Friends.** If a friend or acquaintance in your neighborhood has recently bought or sold a home, ask for a mortgage company recommendation.
- **Online Resources.** Check out the "Resources" section in the back of this book for more information, but you can apply for a loan and find interest rates online at a variety of sites, including E-loan (www.eloan.com), RealEstate.com (www.realestate.com) and Quicken-Loans (www.quickenloans.com).

Charting the Difference!

As you can see below, I have included a fixed-rate and an adjustable-rate mortgage chart for your review. You will quickly notice that fixed-rate mortgages have slightly higher rates compared to the adjustable-rate mortgage, but they also command a tighter spread of

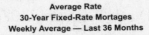

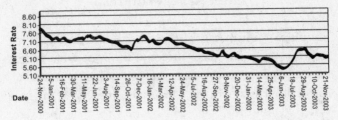

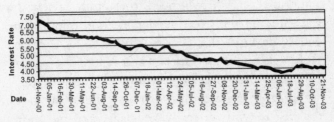

interest rate fluctuations over the thirty-six-month time period—meaning, interest-rate movements go from a low of 5.6 percent to a high of 7.9 percent. Whereas the adjustable rate mortgages have slightly lower rates to begin with, but the spread is much wider—interest-rate movements go from a low of 3.75 percent to a high of 7.25 percent, due to the simple fact that they adjust over time based on current interest-rate fluctuations! More movements mean more implied risk for you over the long term!

Don't Forget to Calculate Your ARM's Interest!

Should you ultimately choose to go with an ARM or hybrid-type loan, make sure you find out what index it is tied to: Treasury bills, certificates of deposit, or some other benchmark. Once you find out what rate system your mortgage will be tied to, remember to note that your rate of interest will be the index rate plus a margin rate charged by your lender for their profit (*markup* in real estate jargon), usually 2.5 percent. However, you will need to carefully review the exact amount with your lender. Keep in mind, many lenders are aware that borrowers tend to focus on the ARM's initial rate of interest and ignore the margin and index that actually determines the loan rate. If you begin to evaluate an ARM based off of the index it is tied to, you are many steps ahead of the game! Remember when it comes to your ARM's full rate to calculate:

Index + Margin = Interest Rate

Questions to Ask Before Taking on an ARM or a Hybrid Loan

- With your current finances, can you still save for retirement if you have a higher mortgage payment to make?

- What does your emergency fund look like? Do you have three to six months of cash on hand to cover living expenses should your mortgage payments increase?

- Can you afford the highest possible payment amounts on the ARM? (Your mortgage broker can tell you what your ARM would be capped at for the lifetime interest-rate cap allowable on the loan.)

- If you *are* stretching to meet the maximum the lender allows you to borrow and testing the limits of your budget, are you in a stable professional position?

- Can you handle the overall mental stress that future rising interest payments could cause you?

Points, Fees, and Appraisal

Now that you are beginning to harness the art of being a mortgage mogul, let's get down to the nitty-gritty part—securing that first-time mortgage. You will want to familiarize yourself with three additional cost areas you will need to know about when it comes to shopping for a mortgage with a lender.

Points

Points are, in fact, rates of interest that your lender will charge you for his work and expense when it comes to processing and approving your mortgage. The good news is that when you buy your home, the points you are charged will be tax deductible. To note, when/if you go to refinance down the road, the total points amount will need to be deducted over the life of the loan rather than upfront. One point is actually one percent of the total loan amount. For example, two points from a $200,000 loan = $4,000. Pretty simple, right? The lender requires you to pay them at the time that you close on your home purchase and begin the journey of repaying your loan.

With a fixed-rate loan and points, you have an inverse relationship. If you can pay more points on a mortgage upfront, your lender should reduce your ongoing interest rate. This type of scenario is most beneficial to you if you don't plan on moving for a long time—the lower the interest rate over the long haul, the better for you in savings!

On the other side of the curve, if you are cash-strapped and want to pay fewer points up front, you can choose to pay a higher ongoing interest rate, as the points will be rolled into the mortgage. This is not such a bad idea for first-time homebuyers—especially if you anticipate that you will only be in your house for a few years. In that case, the strategy of paying less now and more later makes good sense!

The "No-Point" Myth!

Keep in mind that points and interest are trade-offs. If you choose to forego paying points, the rate of interest on your mortgage will be higher. Lenders who push *no-point mortgages* tend to be very aggressive and often offer the least competitive pricing in the mortgage marketplace. No-point loans make sense if you don't plan to own your home for long and are strapped for cash.

A great way to do a little "shopping analysis" of who has the best deal is to ask the different lenders to provide you interest rate quotes at the same point level. For example, you could ask them what their fixed-rate mortgage for thirty years would be at one point.

Fees

Fees are another important area to research when it comes to choosing the right mortgage for you. On top of points, lenders also charge a myriad of up-front fees that you will need to investigate. You want to know exactly how much cash you will need to put down to get that first home.

Once you find a lender to begin to explore working with, ask them to provide, in writing, an itemization of all other charges. Just as lenders offer the no-point loan, they also offer the *no-fee loan,* which, as you probably guessed, works just like the no-point loan. The lender will most likely charge you through a higher ongoing interest rate of the loan.

You will also need to pay a processing or application fee, in the ballpark of $200 or $300. Lenders charge this fee to ensure that you are serious about securing a loan. Plus, they also want to cover their costs should your loan application be rejected. There are a few lenders who don't charge this fee and will return this fee charge should you take their services!

Appraisal

This is a very practical fee. In essence, your mortgage lender wants an unbiased assessment of the property value before they actually take the risk of lending you the money that you agreed to pay for the house. The appraisal usually happens after the seller has accepted your offer on the property.

From the bank's perspective (and from yours too), this appraisal makes sense. If you end up in a financial fiasco or you overpay and home values decline in value, the fear of the lender is that you might leave them stuck with the property. Your appraisal fee is going to be a few hundred dollars, depending on the size, value, and location of the property. If your property is appraised for more than you offered, you'll feel like you got a bargain! If it's appraised for less than you offered and the bank refuses to give you a mortgage for the full amount, you may be able to negotiate with the seller to come down on the price.

In you are on the fence about which type of mortgage will be most attractive to you, try a few on for size. Make sure you talk with professionals or even seasoned family homebuyers who can offer you sound advice given your current financial snapshot, future goals, and overall risk tolerance capacity. Ultimately, you will want to choose a mortgage that feels most comfortable to you in your intuition and allows you to sleep at night, even if that does mean you may have to pay a little extra in interest during the life of the loan.

5

What If I Don't Qualify for a Regular Mortgage?

Creative Financing Techniques for Less-Than-Perfect Credit

Still I am learning.
—Michelangelo

Sheila has OK credit—a few blemishes here and there—but her real issue is the lack of a down payment. She works hard and knows her salary will support a mortgage . . . but it's been impossible to save more than a few thousand dollars. Does she really need 10 percent or even 20 percent down to make the leap into home ownership? Or are there other options available to her?

* * *

Maybe you're self-employed, went bankrupt, have lousy credit history—or no credit history at all. Perhaps you live on disability checks, unemployment—or you have just had a checkered career path thus far. What about just plain not having enough money for a down payment? You feel challenged and intimidated by even the mere thought of qualifying for a conventional mortgage.

Not to worry, you can still make buying your first home a reality. Let's look at some of the other options open to first-time homebuyers today.

How Large of a Down Payment Do I Need?

This is the big question for many first-time homebuyers. Conventional wisdom says that you should aim for a down payment of anywhere from 10–20 percent of the purchase price of the house. This is a good rule of thumb if you're interested in getting a fixed-rate mortgage, as we discussed earlier.

But for other, more creative financing methods, you can get away with much less than that—some of these mortgage programs require as little as 3 percent down! In essence, if you were to buy a home for $150,000, that means you would only need to come up with $4,500, plus closing costs. And if you don't have the closing costs, there are even programs that require nothing down.

Further, if you don't have the money for closing costs, which normally run approximately 3 percent of the purchase price, then oftentimes you will be allowed to come up with those funds through a second mortgage or in some cases the seller can put up the funds (which you can receive as gifts). We'll discuss all of these options and more in this chapter.

Fannie Mae and Freddie Mac

As we discussed earlier, these are the two quasi-public, government-sponsored organizations that are the biggest mortgage lenders in the country that maintain a secondary market in home loans. You may also recall that when you get a loan through a mortgage broker or a bank, chances are that the loan is sold to one of these organizations. In fact, it is estimated that as many as 50 percent of all mortgages go through Fannie Mae or Freddie Mac.

So, to boil it all down, both Fannie Mae and Freddie Mac set the maximum loan you can get, currently about $300,000 (but often adjusted upward), as well as what your FICO score needs to be to get prime loans (around a 680). Not to worry, they also have low- or no-money-down programs as well as programs for those who are credit challenged. Plus, many of their programs are geared to the first-time homebuyer.

As we know from chapter 3, good credit is key. But there are programs such as Freddie Mac Affordable

Are You a First-Time Homebuyer?

Not sure you may qualify as one? Technically speaking, a first-time homebuyer is someone who hasn't owned a home in the last three years.

Merit Rate and Fannie Mae's Timely Payment Rewards mortgage programs that enable you to get mortgages with less-than-stellar credit by paying a higher interest rate than a person with great credit. Usually, the little- or no-money-down payment principles still apply with these programs. The very good news on these programs is that often there are incentive deals that go along with them. One being, if you make twenty-four consecutive payments on time, the interest rate, which ultimately affects the size of your down payment, will be cut.

So, how good does your credit have to be? Freddie Mac and Fannie Mae have guidelines that are along the following: You can't have more than two delinquent payments in the last twelve months or bankruptcies within the last twenty-four months, and no foreclosures within the last thirty-six months. As far as debt is concerned, you may have lots of other types of debt, if you can explain it in terms divorce, medical emergency, job loss, etc.

Generally speaking, you can most likely qualify for one of these mortgages if your monthly payment will be no more than 25 to 30 percent of your gross income (income before taxes) and if your credit history isn't too shabby. The only way to know for real is to go ahead and get yourself preapproved by a mortgage broker. Keep in mind, when it comes to mortgage mathematics with these secondary lenders, is sometimes it is better to have less income than more, because these programs have been especially designed for those of us who otherwise could not afford them!

A good benchmark when it comes to affordability and being an attractive candidate for one of these programs is the median income in your area. For many of these programs you need to earn less than just that. There are exceptions for high-income areas. For example, in California you can earn up to 140 percent of the median income, and in Boston it is 135 percent.

Keep in mind, these programs and their specifications change all the time. My suggestion would be to check directly with secondary lenders to see what programs would work best for you and then plan to contact a mortgage broker or a banker to find out more. Here is their information:

Fannie Mae
3900 Wisconsin Avenue, NW
Washington, DC 20016-2892
202-752-7000
www.fanniemae.com
www.homepath.com

Freddie Mac
8200 Jones Beach Drive
McLean, VA 22102-3110
703-903-2000
www.freddiemac.com

Think of it this way: These mortgages are designed for people who are viewed as good credit risks, but who have simply gotten into some financial trouble. For those of us who have truly bad credit, even though you won't qualify for these programs, there are plenty of other options listed within this chapter, so keep reading!

Local City Governments

As a first-time homebuyer, there are several programs available to you that are administered by your local city government. You will need to contact your city office of housing. What you want to find is what type of programs they offer, the specific qualifications, and how you go about applying. A few key features to these types of programs:

- You must meet certain strict household income guidelines.

- You are limited to the maximum price amount for the home you plan to purchase (this may immediately rule out some buyers in big cities on the West Coast and East Coast due to high prices in those regions).

- You most likely will not get a mortgage directly from these programs, rather you will receive some type of tax credit, insurance, guarantee, or other assistance in qualifying for a home loan.

In essence, you may find extremely helpful assistance in making your first-time home purchase through your local city government, but it will take some legwork on your end that may include not just calling, but also writing or going to government offices to see if you qualify to make it happen. It is definitely worth a day to at least explore your options in this arena. Remember, you only need to find one program that fits your needs and one house that feels like an affordable first home for you!

FHA and HUD

It is important to familiarize yourself with the FHA (Federal Housing Administration), which was originally born out of the Great Depression to help Americans purchase first homes with the first-ever twenty-year long-term financing. The overall reason for creating the FHA was to make housing more affordable to a greater number of people. In fact, the FHA has covered fifteen million American homes since 1934. Since the FHA's inception, the organization has gone through many changes. It is now a part of HUD (U.S. Department of Housing and Urban Development) and is still considered a dominant player in the marketplace.

The major advantage to securing a loan from the FHA is that it provides low down-payment financing with a more lenient perspective on your past credit mistakes. You may secure a home loan for 3 to 5 percent down if you qualify for one of their loans. In stark contrast to Fannie Mae and Freddie Mac, the FHA doesn't actually lend money directly; instead, they insure lenders against their loss. In this situation, if you get an FHA loan from a broker or bank, the FHA will protect the lender if you default on your loan. To contact HUD/FHA for more information on programs, you may contact your state agency or:

HUD
451 Seventh Street, SW
Washington, DC 20410
www.hud.gov
www.hud.gov/offices/hsg./fhahistory.cfm

If you can meet your monthly mortgage payments and you meet the loan's debt-to-income ratios, then you can qualify. FHA loans are specifically known as a great option for people who have few other choices when it comes to buying a home, especially a first home!

Here are a few key features to note to help you get started in this direction should FHA loans sound attractive for your current financial situation:

- No certain income to qualify

- No need to be a first-time buyer

- Need only 2 to 5 percent down if the property is a "single-family home," (which includes: condos, co-ops, townhouses, and multiple-unit buildings with four or fewer units)

- Ability to finance closing costs

- FHA-set limits on the amount lenders can charge for some closing cost fees (e.g., origination of no more than 1 percent of the mortgage)

The not so great characteristics of FHA loans include:

- A maximum loan amount of $115, 200 in low-cost areas and $208,800 in high-cost areas

- A first-time buyer must plan to occupy the property that they buy—they cannot rent

- An FHA appraisal is needed in order to be approved for an FHA loan to ensure that the property is sound, within building code, and free of termites, fungus, erosion, etc.

● A special FHA mortgage insurance must be obtained vs. the regular "private mortgage insurance" (which we will discuss more in the next chapter) required with a Fannie Mae or Freddie Mac loan. You generally pay 2.25 percent of the loan amount up front for it when you take out the loan.

The amount of money you can borrow with FHA loans is restricted, which may negate this opportunity for those of you living on the East or West coast these days. Take a look at the chart below to see if it could work for you:

2003 FHA LOAN LIMITS*

	Standard Limit	High-Cost Areas
Single-Family Home	$154,896	$280,749
Two-Family Home	$198,288	$359,397
Three-Family Home	$239,664	$434,391
Four-Family Home	$297,840	$539,835

*These numbers change frequently based on certain economic variables. Log on to the U.S. Department of Housing and Urban Development for updates at www.hud.gov/ and go to the "Buying a Home" page for more detailed information.

The advantages of an FHA loan are two-fold. One, the restrictions on past credit history problems are more lenient than with other loans. Here is the short list:

- Two years have passed since a bankruptcy.

- It's been three years since you had a foreclosure or deed-in-lieu of foreclosure.

- Any outstanding tax liens have been satisfied.

- All judgments against you have been paid.

The second advantage about FHA mortgages is that they are *assumable*. This means that, if you are buying from someone who has an FHA loan, you can simply take over the loan payments from the seller and save yourself all the bother (and cost!) of securing your own loan. In most cases with a fully assumable FHA loan, there is no appraisal fee, which will save you, the buyer, a good $300 dollars or more. Plus, these loans are a great choice for folks with poor credit or bankruptcies in the past, as the federal government, who underwrites the loans, does not view these historical financial issues of yours in the same light as a private lender. In 2001, 79.5 percent of FHA loans originated with first-time homebuyers.

The ability to assume a loan is also a huge advantage when it comes time to sell. Keep in mind, too, that no other nongovernment or guaranteed loans are assumable. The traditional route for mortgages is that when you eventually sell your property, your current loan will need to be paid off and the next buyer will need to get a new mortgage. With the FHA mortgage, the next buyer can actually take over your existing loan after passing a qualifying process and, if the interest rate you locked in to was fixed at the time you secured the FHA loan, then it is a big plus for the next buyer of your home who will potentially assume the mortgage.

It is important to note that the seller may have some liability for approximately ten years after the sale. Meaning, even if you sell the home, and the buyer defaults, you may be held partially liable for the mortgage. Hence, it is important to make sure you know who you are selling to.

How to Assume an FHA Mortgage

Up until 1986, existing FHA loans were fully assumable. Due to a huge number of foreclosures, the system was amended in 1986 and you must now pass a qualifying process (as mentioned above) before assuming an FHA mortgage from the seller of the home if the FHA loan was issued after 1986. But anyone can qualify to assume an FHA mortgage issued before 1986 with zero credit check! If you have terrible credit, the type of credit that isn't repairable anytime in the near future, finding sellers who have secured an FHA loan prior to 1986 is one of the options available to you. It may not be easy to find this type of mortgage up front, but it is certainly not impossible either. Even though many real estate agents don't know these basic facts, you may still ask for them by name. Be sure to tell your real estate agent that you are looking for a home with an FHA assumable non-qualifying mortgage, and if the agent doesn't know what that means, explain it. Remember, there are still millions of those assumable no-qualifying FHA mortgages out there; you just need to look for them by name!

Regarding your credit history problems, with a potential seller of a home that you are interested in purchasing who has one of these fully assumable no-qualifying FHA mortgages, get organized. Put together a "proactive" file to illustrate to the seller that you are seeking to repair your credit's wobbly ways and that you are definitely worth the risk when it comes to assuming their mortgage. If you can actively illustrate that you are a decent human being who has made a few mistakes but is sincerely seeking to make good on your financial and life responsibilities, you are sure to have a shot at making this happen for yourself.

> *Contrary to the cliché, genuinely nice guys often finish first or very near it.*
> —*Malcolm Forbes*

The Fresh Prince Is Now King of His Castle

Will Smith was famously in deep debt to the IRS early on in his career as a young teen hip-hop artist. Music mogul Benny Medina suggested a sitcom based on Medina's life, about a kid from Philly who comes to California to live with his snooty, rich relatives. The result: NBC's hit sitcom, *The Fresh Prince of Bel-Air*, was born—starring Will Smith! Will has since gone on to publicly discuss his early troubles with managing his money and how he triumphed over his challenges to become the mega-success Hollywood superstar he is today. He is a great example of someone who used his financial struggles as an opportunity to educate himself on how the system works, growing fiscally fit and financially free!

VA Loan

The *VA* stands for Veterans Association. As you may have guessed, this organization was set up to help veterans qualify for home financing. In order to qualify, you had to have been on active-duty status for a minimum number of days during specific periods of time. If you qualify, you are given a certificate of eligibility. This certificate is issued to get your entitlement, which is the amount that the VA will cover. Currently, you can get a VA loan for up to 100 percent or $240,000 maximum. If you buy a home using the VA system and later sell it, you can have the VA reissue your loan. You can then take your entitlement and use it to buy another home. If, however, someone else assumes your VA loan, you may lose your entitlement.

With the exception of the entitlement, VA loans work along very similar lines to the FHA loans. What is important to note for you about VA loans is that just as we discussed earlier in the chapter that FHA loans issued before 1986 are fully assumable, with no qualification process, so too is this the case with VA loans—except they must have been issued on or before May 1, 1988. As with FHA loans, there are millions of homes that are guaranteed by VA loans, and thousands of these no-qualifying assumptions are recorded each year. Hence, you now have two viable options to explore when it comes to qualifying for a mortgage with no credit.

Balloon Loan

As a first-time homebuyer, who most likely is not sitting on a pile of extra cash, a balloon loan/mortgage will probably not be the right option for you. A balloon loan has a fixed interest rate for a set time period, say the first five, seven, or ten years. During that time period you only pay the interest of the loan. But the end of the term of the loan, the whole balance becomes due.

Why are these loans attractive, you ask? It all comes back to the interest rate. Balloon loans start at a lower interest rate, just like ARMs or hybrid loans vs. fixed-rate mortgages. Often buyers choose these loans during high interest rate periods so that they can afford a mortgage.

The big downfall with these loans is that if the loan term expires during a period of high mortgage rates, you may have trouble refinancing the mortgage. This isn't an option for too many buyers . . . except for those who know that they'll sell before the balloon payment is due.

Owner Will Carry Loan

OK, OK, let's say that you just can't find a house for sale that works for you and has one of those tantalizing FHA or VA no-qualifying mortgages available. Or perhaps you may have found one, but the mortgage balance is way below the asking price, and you most definitely don't have the credit to qualify for a new mortgage. Now what?

No need to despair. Another option for making a first-time home purchase happen without great credit is through seller financing. With this scenario, the seller becomes the bank. Each month, instead of writing a check to a bank or a mortgage company, you write that check to the previous owner of your home. With this deal, you own the house just as if you had purchased it with a loan through a bank or mortgage company, except the only person you need to convince to trust you is the seller!

You will want to search through the real estate classified section in your local newspaper to find these types of deals. Look for terms and phrases that include: "owner will carry," "seller financing," "owner may carry," "OWC," or even "OWC 2nd." These are hints that the seller is open to exploring financing themselves.

So, why would a seller want to self-finance? Money! The seller who is open to financing the deal himself or herself stands to make much more money from the actual sale of the house. How does that work? It has to do with how mortgage payments work, which we will discuss at length in the next chapter. However, for now, here is a brief snapshot of how the system works: The majority of mortgages in their early years are more than 90 percent interest, less than 10 percent principal—keep in mind, most mortgages are for thirty-year periods, some fifteen years. If you are paying $1,000 a month to the previous owner of the house, it is pretty likely that more than $900 of it is in interest charges and only $100 or less is going toward your principal balance. Why? Because that is how most mortgages are *amortized* (paid off). The whole mortgage system works in favor of the lender, usually the bank or mortgage company, but in this case it is the seller.

Not sure this makes sense? Check this out! You buy a $100,000 house by putting down 5 percent—$5,000—with a 5.25 percent interest rate over twenty years. Your monthly payment works out to be $950. When you make the first payment of $950, you do not reduce the amount you owe on the house by very much. In fact, less than $2 goes against the principal amount, whereas $948 dollars of the $950 is interest. After your first month's payment, the $95,000 owed is still $94,998. With each month that passes, the proportion of interest goes down and the proportion of principal goes up. Halfway through the twenty years, your $950 monthly payment is equally divided, half to interest and half to principal. If you make the $950 payment every month for twenty years, you will have paid $228,000 on that $95,000 mortgage. Hence, the seller winds up collecting $228,000 for the house versus the $100,000—that is more than double the price of the house, over time.

Wow, right? How about this? If the same $100,000 house, with the same down payment, stretches a $95,000 mortgage over a thirty-year term, the monthly payment goes down to $880, but the final amount paid for the house becomes $316,000!

With owner financing, the property becomes the security for the loan for the seller in case you don't make your payments. At that time the seller would have the option to foreclose on you and take the house back. So, what kind of seller would agree to finance their house? They don't need to be rich, but they have to not need the cash out of their house when selling it. Meaning, many people sell their home, take the equity and use it to purchase another, bigger home. Other people already have a place to move to, and for greater income and possibly tax reasons, they prefer to carry the mortgage.

So, who are the most likely candidates?

Older people who are set to retire or move into a nursing home arrangement. An elderly person may want to be rid of the expense and responsibility of maintaining a home. For them, seller financing provides a comfortable retirement.

Other candidates who may seek seller financing would be homeowners who are in a slow real estate market, because it makes their homes much easier to sell. Look for a house that has been on the market for at least six months; chances are that they would be open to selling with owner financing.

Lastly, if the property is in bad condition—such as a zoning problem, cracked-slab foundation, etc.—no bank will issue a mortgage. The seller may have no choice but to carry the loan. As for this option, be extremely careful. There are entire books that are dedicated to buying rundown homes, but as a first-time homebuyer be careful about exploring this one. Buying a fixer-upper that not even the banks will touch may be biting off more than you can chew the first time out! If you do decide to explore this option, make sure to read additional resources and talk to trusted advisers who will help you accurately assess the cost of addressing the core problems of the home so that you will not have the same problem yourself when you go to sell the house someday.

If seller financing is of interest to you with your

present credit situation, be careful. Make sure to explore this option at length

Talking the Seller into Owner Financing

First, if you find a house that you like that has been listed as "OWC" (Owner Will Carry), all you need to do is convince the seller that you are able to meet their price and terms. However, if you need to convince the seller to carry the financing, you may need to be a little more persuasive. Two suggestions are:

1. **Put the offer in writing.** As in most business dealings, oral or spoken-word agreements do not hold up. This is especially true in real estate. To really get the ball rolling and let the seller know that you are serious, put it in writing.

2. **Show them how they stand to profit.** Many sellers don't realize how much they could get for their home if they simply carried the mortgage themselves. If you demonstrate to the seller how much more money they stand to make, chances are that you will pique their interest. Try including standard amortization tables too, which you can get from your bank—it will look even more professional and may help seal the deal!

Lease with Option

So, what is a *lease with option* you may ask? Simply put, it is a contract between the buyer and seller in which the buyer agrees to rent the home for a specific period of time (normally a year), with a portion or all of the rent going toward the purchase of the property. So, in essence, your rent check that you pay each month is actually going toward building your equity in your home, making the likelihood of buying the place a very good one. With a lease option, you establish the price of the home up front with a contract, so even if the price were to increase during the course of that year, you get the "frozen" price and the seller must comply with the year-old price, potentially making that a bargain for you. Plus, if the value of the home were to decrease in price, with this type of deal, you are not required to exercise your option to buy.

This type of contract is attractive for the seller because it makes their house much easier to sell in a slow market. As for you, the buyer, it makes buying a house more affordable, plus it is much easier to get in without qualifying for a loan and gain some time to find extra financing. Think of it from the lender's point of view, by the time you are looking to option your right to buy the property, you will have paid your rent for one year, having accumulated equity in the property. Hence, you become that much more attractive to qualify for a loan. Better yet, if the owner of the property has seen you demonstrate yourself to be a good tenant who always pays on time, then the seller may even be inclined to finance your purchase—as discussed earlier, "owner financing." Remember, if the seller doesn't need the cash up front, there are *beaucoup* more bucks for the seller to collect in interest. Plus, sellers often don't want the hassle of trying to find a new buyer, which may motivate them to extend you the financing opportunity.

You will most likely not find any homes advertised as lease options in the classified section, but in truth, any house for sale may be available under these terms. Even houses for rent could be lease optioned, if you could just convince the owner to sell to you in this capacity.

The big catch with this type of home purchase arrangement is the down payment, more commonly referred to in this deal as an *option fee*. The option fee required to enter into a lease option agreement is totally negotiable and will often depend on the value of the house. If the house you are looking to purchase is $150,000—it is not unlikely that you will be asked to put down 3 percent of that amount ($4,500). The big reason that this is the downside is not just that you need to potentially come up with the option fee for this deal. If you don't end up exercising your option to buy at the end of the contract term, then you lose your option fee. Keep in mind, there could be no option fee if the seller is desperate or the house is very inexpensive.

The good news about this sort of deal is that some lease contracts build up so much equity that they can actually be sold or transferred, to another buyer. What is important to note is that the original contract can't have a clause that prohibits such a transfer. In fact, the lease with option agreement is truly a type of ownership because it's a legal, binding guarantee of the right to buy a house at a set price, with a certain amount of equity already paid in. For you, the buyer, this is very important, because if your option is very close to expiring and you haven't been able to get the dough for the closing sale, you have the right to transfer the option to a friend or relative with better credit, who could buy the house and then sell it back to you!

Lastly, you have the right to cancel the lease with a thirty-day written notice with no further obligation. But, beware: You will lose all rent credit and your option fee. It gives you, the buyer, the option to change your mind midstream if you truly don't like the house!

Most office stores will carry lease-option purchase forms. You can add your own clauses and make sure that the contract is transferable—and that you have the right to cancel with no penalty. You will want to have a trustworthy real estate agent or attorney review this contract to ensure that everything about it is legal and proper. Finally, a lease option is definitely a form of purchasing that can, in many cases, be done with no credit required. It could be your first step in the door of homeownership and there are multiple ways that it can evolve into a title deed for you without needing a visit to your lending office.

Co-sign

It is a yes-and-no situation. Some lenders will accept a co-signer for your loan, while others won't. If you don't have the credit history, find someone who does and explore working with him or her as a partner to make a mortgage happen for you. Likely candidates include family, relatives, good friends, or even trusted business associates. Plus, if you don't need them for the down payment or to help you with the monthly mortgage payments, then it is that much easier to get someone to co-sign with you.

It is important to appreciate that when someone steps up to co-sign with you, they are held fully accountable should you default on your loan or, worse yet, be foreclosed on. Don't be too disturbed if you are hard-pressed to find someone who will actually say yes to you—this is a big undertaking on his or her part.

One way to entice another person to co-sign is to offer them a deal in which they can participate in an ownership position with the property. If you were to put this person's name on the trust deed or the mortgage, it offers them the opportunity to step in and take over the payments, and possibly save the property, should you stop making payments or go into foreclosure for some reason. In fact, most lenders will request that the co-signer be on the mortgage. Inclusion on the deed is just another formal step to add.

The downside of the co-signer being on the deed is that they now can tie up the property and possibly keep you from selling it. Accordingly, you will want to protect your interests by having an attorney draw up an agreement specifying exactly what interests the co-signer has—none, except in the event that you default. In essence, the agreement will need to detail exactly what say this person has in managing and selling the property and what percent of the profit they will receive when the property is sold—again, none would be the way you will most likely want to go!

Equity Sharing

As the title suggests, this is the sharing of ownership of real property between several parties. There are several different types of equity sharing that may be of interest to you to explore depending on your particular situation. Here are a few to note:

Shared Living Arrangement

In this situation, both parties occupy the property. Ideally, a duplex or even a house with two separate units seems to work best! The investor who put up the greater share of the down payment could live in the larger unit. Another scenario would be that one party pays the full down payment, while the other party puts up their good credit to qualify for the mortgage, then both parties share the mortgage equally. The main idea here is that everything is negotiable with a shared living arrangement. What makes this type of deal so attractive for many single women is the affordability—in many parts of the country, it's astounding. You will want to make sure that you will be shacking up with someone you are compatible with, and trust, before committing to a shared living situation.

Group Purchase

In this situation, a group forms a corporation that acts as a nonprofit membership association to purchase real estate. Each member would hold stock in the corporation and shares of the property. Usually, you would be obligated to offer to sell your stock back to the organization and its members before selling to anyone else. Plus, membership approval would be needed before anyone new could join the group. Going with a group purchase could be a FAB way to get into real property ownership without needing personal credit—because the *group* is granted credit, not the individual. This is a potentially great option for you urban dwellers. In fact, some co-op apartment buildings in New York City have been doing this successfully for years.

In essence, if you have good friends who are eager to stop paying rent, get your assets together and buy!

Credit + Sweat Equity

One unorthodox but interesting twist on the group purchase idea is to "pay" for your share of the property in sweat equity. In this type of arrangement, one party puts up the down payment and their credit, while the other party, who may not have dough or credit to bring to the deal, lives in the house, fixes it up, and pays for the mortgage. As you may be guessing, this is a fixer-upper type of deal. Why would an investor want to participate in a deal like this? One main reason may be the tax advantages. Another is the opportunity to participate in big profits without having to do any work or even make mortgage payments.

The investor and sweat-equity homebuyer strike a deal whereby they agree to sell the home in a fixed time period (usually two to five years for a fixer-upper). Both you and the investor stand to make a chunk of change in profits at that time. Plus, since you will have made the mortgage payments over several years, you most likely have improved your credit situation dramatically. You will also have gotten a start in home ownership, stopped paying rent, and even gotten a few tax breaks!

Foreclosure to You

How the mortgage system works is simple: You give the lender the right to take your home from you and the full right to sell it for the balance due on the mortgage, should you not make your loan, property tax, and homeowners insurance payments. The official legal action to repossess your home and sell it is called *foreclosure*. Hundreds of thousands of homes flood the marketplace for sale each year due to people who fall on hard times (job loss, divorce, death, etc.) or make poor consumer credit choices.

Although buying a first-time home that has been foreclosed on by a lender could potentially amount to huge savings, there are some risks attached. However, given that this particular section in this book is dedicated to the more aggressive measures that you may need to take in order to get into your first home without having all the "traditionally" needed ingredients, it is most definitely worth a review.

There are a few different scenarios that you will want to perhaps explore.

Scenario #1: Buy a Foreclosed Home from a Professional Investor

This first option will be of interest to you if you have little or no credit or money for a down payment. Professional investors, with lots of cash on hand and good credit, can swoop in and buy foreclosed and distressed properties at bargain-basement prices. These professional investors attend the court foreclosure auctions and pick up good houses for a fraction of their value. The professional then turns around and sells it to you, the buyer who has inadequate credit and/or financing. Just closing costs are needed to seal the deal. In essence, the investor finances the purchase so you don't have to qualify at a bank or mortgage company.

The big note of caution with this scenario: You need to be extra careful about who you do the deal with to make certain they are credible and not scam artists. You will want to do some fact-checking with the Better Business Bureau in your area before signing over any closing costs to them. Remember that these people specialize in buying homes that have been foreclosed and that they will not hesitate to foreclose on you should your payments fall behind. Having said that, exploring this type of deal may offer you a way to stop paying rent and get into home ownership without paying a down payment. If you can meet the terms, definitely make the payments, and have safe legal title of the property—it might be worth it for you!

Scenario #2: Buy a Forclosed Home from a Bank or Lender

A second option, which is considered much safer, is to buy the foreclosed home directly from the lender/bank who has called in the home loan, known now as an REO (Real Estate Owned). It is now the lender/bank offering it to the public. Keep in mind that buying foreclosed property is considered the domain of real estate investors. Having said that, it does not mean that a first-timer couldn't go in and get a terrific bargain. However, in this scenario, you would need cash up front to buy the home outright in the bidding process that would take place at auction. My suggestion would be to read more books that focus solely on buying homes in foreclosure before moving forward with bidding on a house by yourself.

The major pitfalls associated with foreclosed homes in general have to do with buying the previous owner's problems, and could include the following, which you should be aware of in either of the scenarios just discussed:

- **Physical**—Homeowners may act with total vengeance due to the emotional devastation of being foreclosed upon. This could result in them stripping the house before they leave: taking appliances, wall or light fixtures, sinks, toilets, etc. They could also do a lot of damage, even pouring concrete down the sink or breaking windows. Lenders will not always let you inspect foreclosed property prior to auction. Hence, the great risk of buying foreclosed property at an auction or from a professional investor: Not being able to first inspect the property, the costs may greatly exceed the reward. Having said that, you will want to make sure that you make it a priority to purchase only a first-time home whose property you can have inspected prior to purchase.

- **Possession**—This is a worst-case scenario, but worth noting. You could buy your foreclosed home to find that the previous owners are still living in it with their last remaining possessions. It will be your responsibility to evict them.

Distressed Seller

The title certainly keeps it simple. Finding a distressed seller can be magic. You may have the opportunity to get your first-time home purchase at a bargain basement price. This could mean moving into the neighborhood of your choice, which previously might have looked incredibly unaffordable for your first home purchase. So, what are the telltale signs of a desperate seller? When you hear sound bites such as, "I am being driven out of town," "I haven't had any work in six months," "I can't find a job," "They are on my case" (meaning the lender, of course!), bingo—you may have a great opportunity on your hands. That said, the slow real estate months of the year are during the wintertime, November through December specifically. That is because of the holiday season, and people generally don't want to move during cold months. This could be your opportune time to find more capacity in the marketplace for homes with less competition, but even more desperate distressed sellers at the same time!

Back on the Market (BOM) Properties

When a listed house receives an acceptable offer, the seller will most likely instruct their agent to not to actively market the property or take other offers while they fine tune the deal with the buyer. This could include the property inspection and the arranging of financing to satisfy the contract terms and conditions of sale for the property. However, oftentimes property comes back on the market for a number of reasons, including the buyer's cold feet or insufficient funds; the lender deciding the house wasn't worth as much as the buyer wanted to pay, thus turning them down for the loan; or perhaps it was an inspection issue. As a result, when the house comes back on the market with the BOM attached to the listing, it gets a bad rap in the general marketplace.

Who wants something that has been picked over and passed on? BOM homes on average sell at a lower price when listed for a second time. Having said that, if you find a BOM, find out why it has come back on the market. If it was a property defect, have the seller provide inspection reports stating that the problem has been fixed. Remember too, sellers who have had a deal go sour are more humble when it comes to price and terms with the next buyer. It is a potential win-win situation for you to explore.

30/70 Rule

The final option to wrap this chapter up with is the plain and very simple 30/70 rule. You won't exactly find it written anywhere, but it is worth noting for the severely credit challenged who don't qualify. It is a common practice in lending circles that if you can come up with 30 percent of the down payment for your house, the lender most likely will issue a mortgage for the remaining 70 percent. The logic being that if someone can pay 30 percent, it is highly unlikely that they will walk away from the investment! It is a huge commitment, which in most cases will override bad credit-history issues.

As you can see, there are many creative financing opportunities available to you today to make your first home purchase a reality NOW. You should feel incredibly enthused about the infinite possibilities to aid you in owning a piece of the American Dream. The more you focus your attention on what you want and begin exploring creative ways to achieve it, the more opportunity will be consistently knocking on your door.

Now that you know you have huge flexibility and a plethora of options to explore when it comes to working around either poor credit history or minimal funds for a down payment or closing costs, let's move ahead to the next chapter so you can figure out the best ways to master a mortgage that is right for you.

6

Should I Work with a Real Estate Agent?

Assembling Your Posse of Professionals to Seal the Deal

*It's seizing the day and accepting responsibility for your
future. It's seeing what other people don't see, and
pursuing that vision no matter who tell you not to.*
—*Howard Schultz, Starbucks*

*Wendy was an apartment dweller in Cincinnati who had
been dreaming of owning her own home ever since last year,
when three of her friends bought homes in that city. Before
Wendy approached her friends' real estate agents, she did
some homework on her own. Wendy not only went to town
on her credit report, making minor adjustments that would
increase her scoring, she also spent some time reviewing and
even driving around neighborhoods that she had calculated
were within her budgeted home purchase amount. Then, she
took time to meet with each of the three real estate agents referred by her three friends.*

Upon final review, Wendy chose to go with Norma, who

was referred by her girlfriend Alida. Due to Wendy's due diligence and preparation, she had an amazing process of searching for, finding, bidding on, and closing on her first home purchase. Wendy is not only thrilled about her choice and her new home, she is also appreciative at how uncomplicated her home shopping experience turned out to be!

* * *

At this point, you are hopefully feeling inspired and invigorated by how truly possible it is to become a first-time homebuyer. You know how much house you can afford, how to get your credit ready for the scrutiny of a mortgage application, and you know about all of the different mortgage options available to you . . . regardless of whether your credit is spotless or a bit tarnished.

Your next task will be to create a strong real estate team—a group of professionals you can trust to help you find your dream home and get you the best deal possible. The three key components to any first-time buyer's team are: a mortgage broker, a real estate agent, and the Internet. When we finish this chapter, you will be totally equipped and confident to begin perusing real estate listings to find your dream home!

Mortgage Broker vs. Mortgage Lender

Back in chapter 2, we talked about the difference between getting prequalified and getting preapproved for a loan. If you've been doing your homework, you've been exploring your options a bit. But how do you find a great lender to fill your needs? It's time to get a mortgage broker or mortgage banker on your team.

Mortgage Broker

A *mortgage broker* is a company or individual who brings together borrowers and lenders, takes loan applications, processes the papers, and then submits files to an institutional investor once a deal is reached. A mortgage broker is your agent when dealing with a savings and loan (S&L), credit union, bank, or mortgage banker—all of whom would potentially underwrite your loan. Mortgage brokers tend to work with a huge assortment of investors who buy loans on the secondary market. These investors specialize in providing mortgage bankers and brokers with an enormous supply of money to create new mortgages, with which they can offer a wide variety of loan packages to buyers like you.

Mortgage Banker

These people are also involved with the "origination of the loan" side of the business, but they take it to the next level, which is that they also get involved with servicing the loan and closing on the loan in their own name with their own funds. A good example would be if a bank loaned you the money for your first home with the bank's own stash of cash. When you closed on the loan, the same bank might service your account, collect payments, and make sure your real estate taxes were being paid. Alternatively, the company could sell your loan on the secondary market to institutional investors and then relend the money.

So, what is the big difference you need to note? Mortgage bankers not only make their money on actually making you a loan to buy your home, in which you pay fees and points, but they have the opportunity to make additional money on the spread between the loan and the going rate of the loans in the secondary market. Meaning, if they loan you a thirty-year, $100,000 mortgage at 6 percent and are then able to sell it on the secondary market for 6.5 percent—the mortgage banker is going to make an additional .5 percent on the loan or $14,000 in real dollars!

Although mortgage brokers are technically the "guys in the middle," they can, in effect, be your personal shopper. For the first-time homebuyer, there are several compelling reasons why working with a mortgage broker can be a good bet when it comes to finding the right lender and mortgage for you.

For one, mortgage brokers have the opportunity to shop the entire universe of mortgage loans in existence to find the best loan for you. Fair pricing and the art of great deal-making are always determined by how many players are competing for your business. Mortgage brokers can also be incredibly helpful in explaining the mega myriad of choices of different loans available to you and guiding you through all the different paperwork you will need to sift through to make a loan happen.

As not all of us having sterling credit and a ton of cash to plop down to secure a first-time mortgage from a lender, a mortgage broker is more likely to help you prepare and possibly polish a loan application, while also directing you toward certain lenders who would make you a loan given your specific challenges. In essence, mortgage brokers are well versed in making deals on your behalf with lenders who don't really want to deal with credit-challenged borrowers or those who seek to borrow 90 percent or more up front for the price of the home they seek to purchase. If you are like most first-time homebuyers today and have these specific challenges, keep in mind that the shady brokers out there who try to charge insane interest rates and points to inflate their commission seem to prey on borrowers who have credit challenges and other qualification issues.

How Much for a Mortgage Broker, You Ask?

Mortgage brokers will charge you anywhere from .5 percent to 2 percent of the total loan value to utilize their expert services. The points and fees that you pay a mortgage broker are usually the same as what you would pay a lender or a mortgage banker. Why? Lenders are agreeable to sharing their normal fees with an outside mortgage broker who is not employed by the bank. They deduce that if you got the loan from the bank directly, you would still be taking up the time of the bank's employees.

Second, the other good part is that the mortgage broker you choose to work with is allowed to negotiate their commission. It is not unusual for a mortgage broker to lower his commission on a deal in order to make it happen. Remember, a broker doesn't get paid unless the deal gets done. Hence, it is completely reasonable to assume that you have the upper hand in negotiating your broker's commission rate when finally cutting a deal with a lender. It is your hard-earned money and you are the central hub to the deal—don't be shy about negotiating!

Having said all that, brokers operate like car salespeople, insurance salespeople, or stockbrokers. It is their job to sell mortgages and make commissions. In actuality, that is a good thing for you too! Why? Because they have a true vested interest in making you happy by finding a great deal for your mortgage, so that you can close and they can get their commission. Do remember, though: It is your responsibility to find a broker you can build good rapport with, who genuinely wants to help you find the right lender and make your first-time home purchase happen for you.

Tips for Finding the Right Mortgage Broker

Now that you have good understanding of how mortgage brokers work, here are some friendly tips on how to find a great broker who makes you feel comfortable, respected, and sure of getting a good deal. I suggest you chat with at least three brokers and interview at least two.

- **Ask family and friends.** This will be your first place to explore: Find anyone who is house hunting, owns a newly purchased home, or has a client or friend who has worked with a great broker recently. Remember to ask why they liked the broker.

- **Ask your employer, colleagues, and professional organizations.** Any of these might have or know of a relocation service that could provide you with a good referral.

- **Ask other real estate professionals.** Not only real estate agents but tax, legal, and financial advisers. Keep in mind that these people may have a vested interest in pointing you toward a specific direction.

A few good questions to ask a prospective mortgage broker:

- **Do they do deals with little or nothing down?** For obvious reasons, we single, solvent-but-not-yet-loaded gals need a broker who is fairly fluent in mortgage lending—with terms that include the little- or no-money-down scenario. If your potential broker isn't, time to say "NEXT!"

- **How many clients does the broker do business with?** You want a broker who has a cap on how many clients they are servicing at one time, to ensure that you will have the appropriate amount of time you need to work with them to find the right lender for you.

- **How many lenders does the broker work with?** You want a broker to have a multitude of lenders who do business with them. Remember, your broker is your personal shopper. His job is to pick the right lender for you.

- **How does the broker keep up to speed with the new mortgage programs out there?** You want your broker to have a good sense of all the different changing packages available in the mortgage market. It is not a good sign if you find your prospective broker is insistent about a few programs, yet will not explain others in detail when asked.

Rounding up a Real Estate Broker

Start with good people, lay out the rules, communicate with them, motivate them, and reward them. If you do all those things effectively, you can't miss.
—*Lee Iacocca*

Ok—by now you have shopped around town for a maverick of a mortgage broker who has preapproved you for a loan from a lender—and now you know how much you can afford when it come to shopping for your first house. Excellent work! Your next key player on your property posse includes a real estate broker or real estate agent.

Brokers and agents are different, but both are well qualified to help you with your real estate needs. Both are real estate professionals who must take classes and be accredited; a broker has taken additional classes and has passed additional accreditation to receive their broker's license. No matter whether you choose to work with a broker or an agent, make sure they are licensed by your state (you can ask to see their license, or you can check with your state licensing bureau).

Your first home purchase will most likely be the biggest single investment you have ever made. You definitely need someone to work with you who has extensive knowledge of property values, especially in the area you are looking to buy! Just as your mortgage broker shopped around and found you the best deal on a mortgage, your real estate broker or agent will act on your behalf to find you the right property. The real estate agent you choose to be a part of your property posse will need to help you accomplish four things:

1. Find you a first home that fits your specifications.

2. Be able to tell you what the home is worth.

3. Help supervise property inspections.

4. Help negotiate on your behalf to make sure that you don't overpay for the house of your choice.

In truth, a good agent's knowledge base of property values and nifty negotiating skills could literally save you thousands of dollars on your first home purchase. Let's say that there is a house that has a worth of $100,000 and you have a good agent working for you who knows that you are in no hurry to buy. With their insight, you might be able to purchase that house for less than the asking price. Alternatively, let's say the seller has a better agent than you do and you are actually itching to buy that same house—you might end up paying even more than the asking price for the property. Home prices are always directly related to the buyer's and seller's motivation, need, and knowledge. But, another big part of this deal-making process truly comes down to the real estate agent's knowledge of what comparable houses have sold for and their nifty negotiating skills.

Real Estate Agent: Friend or Foe?

The truth is, many first-time buyers have a significant "fear factor" when it comes to real estate agents. Maybe you've visited a few agents' offices and have been treated with little interest or respect. Some single women buyers comment that they don't get taken as seriously by real estate agents as their male friends do, or as their friends buying as a couple. Perhaps you've heard a horror story about an unscrupulous real estate agent. Many first-time buyers fear that real estate agents just want them to buy homes that cost more than they can afford, and that agents just want a quick sale to ensure their own commission check!

You should never be made to feel inferior by an agent, and you should never feel like you're being taken advantage of. The honest real estate professionals are out there! In the following sections, we are going to discuss how to find a "good apple" real estate agent vs. a bad one. Remember, just as you are the head honcho when it comes to mortgage brokers and lenders, so too are you when it comes to reeling in the right real estate agent. You run the show! If you bring a high level of energy and enthusiasm to all your first-time home negotiations, you will increase your chance of not only getting a great deal, but also of having fun with the whole exciting adventure.

How Your Real Estate Agent Will Get Paid

In order to empower yourself to create a win–win relationship with your real estate agent, it is vital that you first understand how the system works—meaning, how your real estate agent will get paid.

The key word here is *commission!* Real estate agent commissions are calculated based on the percentage of the sale price of a home. Depending on what type of agents are negotiating on your and the seller's behalf, the commission could be anywhere from 1 percent to 7 percent. The exciting news is that you, as the buyer, are not technically responsible for paying this cost in addition to the sale price of the house, loan charges, property inspection fees, homeowner's insurance premium, moving costs, etc. The commission paid to both buying and selling agent is paid out of the seller's pocket. In effect, it may appear that the commission comes out of both the seller's and buyer's pockets but, in fact, it is the seller that pays the commissions. Let's say the Joneses seek to sell a piece of property for approximately $100,000. The Joneses will then put up the same piece of property to sell for $120,000. This will offer the Joneses a little wiggle room in price negotiations with a future buyer and assure them that the real estate commission of, say, 6 percent is factored in. This is important to keep in mind when you are looking at houses for sale: The price is always negotiable!

Another compelling reason the price on a home is always negotiable is that real estate commissions are negotiable too. Real estate agents don't get paid unless the property sells. In fact, the contract (listing and purchasing agreements, in real estate jargon) that property owners or buyers sign with a broker to sell or buy a piece of property simply states that by the enforcement of state law the commissions are not fixed and may be negotiated between sellers and brokers.

The commissions that the buying and selling agents receive are distributed to them at the closing of escrow (which we will discuss in chapter 7). In the preceeding example, let's say the Joneses sold their home at their ideal listed price of $120,000 with a real estate–agents' commission of 6 percent. That would mean that both the buying and the selling agent would split the $12,000 commission to each receive $6,000.

It will be equally as important for you to also know how your real estate agents' commission is ultimately paid out to them net dollars. If the buying agent you choose to work with is a part of a real estate brokering house, such as Coldwell Banker or Century 21, their brokerage firm will most likely take 50 to 70 percent of the commission they receive from your real estate transaction. Meaning, with the example above of the Joneses, the buying agent would only receive $3,000 of the $6,000 commission from the transaction if their final take was a 50 percent deal. In other firms, like RE/MAX, your real estate agent will pay a fixed monthly fee to the brokerage firm they work with, which means they most likely keep a greater portion of the commissions they bring in the door. Generally, the amount is approximately 80 percent to 90 percent. Considering again the example of the Joneses, the buying agent would receive $4,800 of the $6,000 commission from the transaction if their final take was 80 percent of the deal. Agents who work on their own as independent brokers are not required to split their commissions with anyone.

Buyer Beware: Three Types of Agent Relationships to Note

1. **Buyer's Agent.** These agents work only for the buyer. The important part to understand is that the buyer's agent never works for the seller, even if the buyer's agent receives a commission from the seller. How does the buyer's agent receive a commission from the seller, you ask? As discussed, a buyer's agent receives a commission that is tied to a percentage amount that the buyer spends for the property, which is ultimately paid by the seller for the monies received for selling their house. No matter how you slice this pie, there will always be an inherent conflict of interest as a buying agent because their commission size is always going to be dictated by how much the buyer paid for the house!

2. **Seller's Agent.** This is where the agent works only for the seller.

3. **Dual Agent.** There are two forms of dual agency:

DUAL AGENCY, PART I: This first type of dual agency is where two different agents from the same agency work for both the seller and the buyer in a property transaction. So, even though two different agents are involved, the key point is that both agents work for the same real estate brokering company. If you choose a small agency, chances are this will not happen to you. If you choose a big agency like Coldwell Banker or Century 21, it's much more likely. There are two major concerns that you should be aware of. First, that your agent absolutely isn't sharing confidential information about you, the buyer, with any of the colleagues at his/her agency. Second, that with this type of dual agency, an agent might push their own in-house listings because they, in fact, get a higher commission on those listings than on outside listings. It is legally required that dual agency be disclosed to you as the buyer. If it goes undisclosed, it is possible to actually have a purchase agreement revoked.

DUAL AGENCY, PART II: The second form of dual agency is where one agent acts on behalf of both the buyer and the seller. In fact, there is a growing trend with the new, young group of real estate agents that are cropping up around the country that, in effect, allows both the buyer and the seller to save money on their property transaction and to each net more at the closing table. For example, Help-U-Sell, a national real estate company that specializes in dual agency—

one agent for both the buyer and seller—makes deals that work like this: A property is sold for $200,000. Normally, the commission for a traditional company is 6 percent, which equals a total of $12,000 in commissions. With a Help-U-Sell agent who listed the same property and sells it for $200,000, the commissions are much less. As a dual agent, the Help-U-Sell agent represents both the buyer and seller in the transaction. The fee to list the home is $2,950, charged to the seller. The difference in dual agent commission to the seller vs. a traditional seller's broker is a whopping $9,050. Even if the buyer haggles a little and gets the price slightly reduced, both parties still win. If the Help-U-Sell dual agent agrees with the seller to accept $195,000, the buyer saved $5,000 on the price of the property. But the seller still "walks away" with $4,050 MORE than the she would have with the traditional company.

The Help-U-Sell dual agent was able to sell the home faster for the seller because of the flexibility in price *and* saved the buyer $5,000. Now, this is what I like to call a win-win negotiation! As Scott Haggerty, owner of Help-U-Sell in St. Louis, Missouri, said, "I very much like dual agency because it eliminates one agent from the verbal and emotional aspects of a real estate transaction. The process of negotiating an offer with the seller and buyer is actually a reasonably easy one. A dual agent knows exactly what the seller wants and the agent also knows what the buyer is capable and willing to offer for the property."

It is crucial that a dual agent not disclose any information about the buyer that would put the buyer at a disadvantage to the seller, just as you must not disclose any information about the seller that would put the seller at a disadvantage to the buyer. Such as, the agent knowing the buyer would increase the initial offering price to a certain amount and knowing the seller would have accepted less than the initial offering from the buyer. Ultimately, the total savings in commissions create a potential win-win savings for both the buyer and seller in a real estate transaction, which could make the difference in affording that fabulous first home or not. **Be open to dual agency, but also be careful.** The quality, expertise, and integrity of an agent are important. Please note: Dual agency is not permitted in all states.

Make a Deal with Your Buying Agent

Should you choose to shy away from working with any type of dual-agent scenario, another option you may want to explore with your prospective buyer's agent is to negotiate a preplanned deal with your realestate agent. Remember—commissions are usually negotiable! Make them an offer they can't refuse. If you know that you budgeted to buy a house for no more than $150,000, and your agent normally gets a commission of 3 percent, then offer them a straight up-front commission of $4,000 and an extra $100 for every $1,000 they can reduce the property price in the final sale. This is called a *lump-sum commission* with an incentive bonus—another win-win situation. Of course, this approach only works if you are certain about the amount you are willing to spend in buying your first home!

Multiple Listing Service (MLS)

Many real estate agents work together to buy and sell property through choosing to work with one another through membership in a Multiple Listing Service (MLS). Once these real estate agents from different agency offices share this information, in essence, they are then subagents (*cooperating agents,* in real estate jargon), who are required to try to get top dollar for the property they are selling. If you and your buying agent find yourselves dealing with a cooperating agent on a piece of property, look closely at the price tag.

Tips for Finding Your Real Estate Agent

Now that you have good understanding of how real estate agents work, here are some friendly tips on how to find the right real estate broker for you. Just like with a mortgage broker, chat with at least three and interview at least two.

1. **Ask your mortgage broker.** By now, you will have begun creating a good working relationship

with your mortgage broker and been preap-proved for a loan. Remember, your mortgage broker only gets paid if you find an appropriate house within your budget and lock into a loan from a lender. It is in your mortgage broker's ut-most interest to give you a few great referrals when it comes to finding a great real estate agent. Make sure to ask your mortgage broker if there are any kickbacks they receive from mak-ing this reference. If so, it doesn't necessarily mean that it is a deal breaker, it is just good to be well-informed of the exact understanding in place before choosing to do business with some-one along these lines. You will also want to ask your mortgage broker if he can put you in touch with other buyers who have recently bought from his recommended agents, whom you could call upon as a reference.

2. **Ask family and friends.** This will be your sec-ond place to explore. Find someone who is cur-rently house hunting, owns a newly purchased home, or owns property in your prime location for buying your first piece of property—as there is a good chance they will know of real estate agents who could work well for you. Always re-member to ask why they liked the broker they refer for you!

3. **Ask your employer, colleagues, professional or-ganizations.** Any of these entities could have or know of a relocation service that could give you a good referral.

4. **Ask related professionals.** Tax, legal, and financial advisers plus escrow officers could give you a referral.

5. **Research newspapers.** Check out the "Real Estate" section to see which real estate agencies seem the largest or most well-established in your area. Hint: They're probably the ones with the biggest ads every week.

Six Characteristics of a Great Agent

1. Great agents have extensive experience in working with the first-time homebuyer. They can work with you even if you're cash strapped and have little money for a down payment.
2. Great agents always have time to help you understand the step-by-step process of buying your first home.
3. Great agents work full time, not part time as they try to transition into becoming a real estate agent.
4. Great agents are never pushy and offer you ample time to decide what is right for yourself and ultimately support your decisions—after all, it will be you left to live in the home!
5. Great agents choose to work within a certain location and property type so that they can be masters of their craft.
6. Great agents have great contacts who offer you reasonable rates and good leads on everything from title officers to property inspectors to lawyers to government officials.

Venturing Out with an Activity List

Once you have identified a few good candidates to interview as prospective real estate agents, you will want to ask for their activity list. The activity list is a list of every property the agent listed or sold during the last year. It is sort of like a report card and it is a superb way to cut to the finer points of how good a fit this prospective agent may be to suit your needs. Seasoned agents happily give you their activity list and references for your review.

What to Look for on the Activity List?

- **Buyers vs. Sellers**—Great seasoned agents tend to work half with buyers and half with sellers. Keep in mind: Newer agents tend to work just with buyers. Agents who only work with sellers may not have the chops to do the right job for you as a buyer.

- **Price**—Does the agent deal with your price range? You will want to find someone who does; it will be helpful making sure they have time for you.

- **Type of Property**—Does the agent deal in single-family homes? If they work with co-ops more, you might want to look elsewhere.

- **Location Focus**—Does the agent restrict to a certain geographic focus? If so, is it your area of choice territory for your first home? If so, good!

- **Reference Information**—Get contact information of current buyers/sellers; you will want to use these buyers as a reference tool later on.

Five Qualities You Want from Your Agent

- You want your agent to represent you solely as a buying agent only, unless *you* choose to work with a dual agent like Coldwell Banker or a discounted dual agent like Help-U-Sell. Should the first form of dual agency arise during your process of finding your first home with a buying agent, as discussed earlier, you will want to be informed right away.

- You want to work with an agent committed to keeping up with the times. Perhaps agents who have recently taken real estate courses or have even offered them themselves to help them stay on their toes.

- You want to make sure the *real estate agent* is going to be available to you, not his or her assistant. If an assistant is involved, find out exactly how much time the real estate agent plans to be available to you in the process and if you feel the assistant is qualified to work with.

- You want a real estate agent who has at minimum one year on the job; five is a good benchmark to shoot for. But remember, this is about common sense and gut instincts on your part. Time on the job is absolutely no guarantee of ability to perform the job at hand!

- You want an agent that is not representing more than five to six clients at a time to ensure that the agent will have an appropriate amount of time available to handle your listing. This is a ballpark number and you can always ask them if they believe they will have the time available to service your needs as a first-time home buyer.

Checking References

Although each activity list may include as many as forty or fifty transactions, you won't need to call each one to get an accurate read on your prospective real estate agent. Here is an easy three-step process to follow that will serve you well in time efficiency and the gathering of critical information so that you can make an informed decision.

1. Since you are the buyer, only review the buying deals—you just shortened your list by a good 30 to 50 percent.

2. Focus on finding people from the list who bought property along the lines of what you are looking to buy with regards to: location, property type, and price value.

3. Call two buyers who purchased property within the last six to twelve months and two buyers who closed escrow within the last three months.

Final Note on Finding the Right Real Estate Agent

Buying your first home is an excellent adventure, but it is stressful too! Do you like the agent? Do your personalities jibe? Do you kind of "get" each other? Is there a good, natural resonance and synergy? Do you sense an intuitive level of trust? Do you feel they are qualified to do a good job for you? Do you have good communication? Do you feel they really listen to what you are saying? Would you feel proud to have this individual representing you?

Once you have reviewed your two or three prospective real estate agents' activity lists and talked with them—and their former buying clients—make sure you take the time to ask yourself the above questions. As a first-time homebuyer, you will definitely need some handholding and a really strong and knowledgable real estate agent. Take the time to go with what feels right vs. what might look right for you. You want to equip yourself with the best property players available to you in order to get the best deal on your first home!

The Internet as a Real Estate Tool

In order to complete your perfect posse of property players, you will want to include the Internet on your team from the start. Let's face it: the first thing you probably did when you started to think about buying a home was to go online and start researching. That's all well and good, and online resouces and realty sites have definitely made home buying a much easier experience in many ways. But do remember that the Web is ultimately a *selling* tool for a myriad of businesses whose objective is to capture your attention, and then your business. Take all the info you get online with a grain of salt. When it comes to buying your first home, nothing can compare to getting a sense of your prospective neighborhood, property, and the people who currently inhabit it by making several visits to the area itself.

Still, the Internet has some incredible information for you as a first-time homebuyer, including: comparative analysis of home prices, communities, school districts, and crime statistics. You will also want to explore mortgages, real estate agents, grants and government assistance, home insurance quotes, home inspectors, and movers.

Given that there is an overwhelming supply of varied information on the Web, let's break it down into three different categories:

1. Internet Shopping for Loans

2. Internet Shopping for Homes

3. Real Estate News

Internet Shopping for Loans

Once you find a mortgage broker, get preapproved, find a real estate agent, and find the first home you want to buy, you will want to consider doing some comparative analysis on the Web to double check what else is out there—to ensure that what you were offered by your broker is an absolutely competitive deal compared to what other lenders are offering. Plus, if it happens that you end up finding a better deal on your own, you will want to check back with your mortgage broker to see whether they can match it.

www.eloan.com—This website is often referenced as one of the best for online shopping for a home loan. There are great tools on this site that allow you to easily compare the cost of different loans with various lenders.

www.homepath.com—Fannie Mae, which we discussed in chapter 2, is a secondary mortgage lender that backs a majority of your local mortgage lenders. "Homepath" is a new section on their site that is dedicated to homebuyers and homeowners and offers expanded content, tools, and resources, all in one convenient portal.

www.hsh.com—This is a great website to review analytical data and statistics on historical and current mortgage rates. You can find helpful additional comparative analysis on mortgages, such as: fixed rates, ARMs, and hybrid ARMs when it comes to buying your first home!

www.norwest.com—Norwest is a large national mortgage company that offers excellent information on what mortgages are available to you.

Internet Shopping for Homes

Once you have found a piece of tempting real estate, or even before you have located the right one for you, it sure doesn't hurt to get jazzed up about what is actually out there, on the market, available to you in your price range. There is nothing like actually seeing something you like to motivate you to move forward with making a first-time home purchase! Plus, the more you are aware of what is out there on the market that is affordable for you with your specifications, the easier it will be for both you and your real estate agent to find the right fit of a first home for you.

www.realtor.com—This website has well over one million listings from the Multiple Listing Service (MLS), which we discussed earlier in this chapter. The site is sponsored by the National Association of Realtors.

www.homes.com, www.homeseekers.com, and www.cyberhomes.com—All of these websites have fairly extensive selections of home listings. Be fore-warned: Many listings contained in these websites can be incomplete or even outdated—be sure to be thorough so that you do not waste time when checking them out.

www.helpusell.com, www.ziprealty.com, www.erealty.com, and www.owners.com—These websites are mainly dedicated to the folks who are trying to sell their property on their own, or are looking to work with a discount broker or dual agent who will charge them less than traditional real estate brokers. They are worth checking out, as their prices may be more competitive for you as a buyer since the seller does not have to pay as much in commission going this route.

Real Estate News

There are a few government organizations and other useful links that can help you find useful real-time real estate news and information that you will find helpful!

www.bea.doc.gov—This website offers you local economic data from the U.S. Department of Commerce's Bureau of Economic Analysis.

www.ashi.com—The web site can help you find a certified ASHI (American Society of Home Inspectors) inspector for your first home, which we will discuss more at length in chapter 7. This site offers helpful information on consumer protection issues.

Now that you know how to pull together your posse of property players—including a maverick of a mortgage broker, a regal real estate agent, and the wonders of the World Wide Web—time to begin searching (if you haven't already!). Let's find your dream home.

7

Where Should I Look?

Insider Tips for Finding Great Deals—
from Manhattan to Main Street, USA

*The kind of people who get on in this world are the
people who get up and look for the circumstances they
want, and, if they can't find them, make them.*
—George Bernard Shaw

Samantha is one of those no-nonsense kind of girls. She is
all about finding the good deals and is prepared to hunt for
them, too. When Samantha decided to purchase her first
home, she scoured the "Real Estate" section for a few
months, did a bit of online research, and actively drove
around different neighborhoods taking notes. It was absolutely no surprise to any of her friends when she landed a
fabulous first home deal in an "up and coming" section of the
city that has ended up seeing incredible price appreciation in
the two years since she bought.

Upon request by Samantha's girlfriends, she revealed her
biggest success secret to buying a great first home with tons of
appreciation potential: "Use your common sense, be ready to
hustle a bit, and focus on finding a location that has yet to
be 'discovered' as the IT neighborhood." Samantha used her

keen bargain-hunting habits and applied them to her first home purchase experience too!

* * *

Time to start making your shopping list! In this chapter we're going to start writing up your wish list—along with a bit of a real-world reality check—by helping you understand what would be most reasonable to ask for when shopping for your first home. Plus, to keep you ahead of the game, I am going to help you start thinking about how much you will get for your first-time home purchase when you go to sell it. Remember: The best time to start thinking about how much money you can make from your first home purchase is when you go to buy it. If you don't let your excitement for buying your first home blind you to its flaws in the eyes of the next potential buyer, then you have a much greater chance of actually buying a great home *and* getting a smart deal.

Statistics from the National Association of Realtors reveal that today, on average, renters and homeowners live in their homes only about five to seven years. Plus, appreciation in your home's value will create amazing equity (the difference between the market value of your home and the actual amount you owe on your mortgage) that can be incredibly useful in the future for you besides just increasing your net worth. If you don't decide to trade up to a bigger home, you could start a business, go back to school, or even travel around the world! There are no guarantees that your home will increase in value at all, but statistics do reveal that home prices, on average, increase 3 to 5 percent per annum—and in metropolitan cities that number tends to be much higher. By seeking to buy a good home in an equally good neighborhood, you will automatically increase your chances of making money in a strong or weak property market.

Having said all that, keep in mind that property prices are always fluctuating due to factors beyond your control: interest rates, cyclical economic factors, job markets, and supply/demand for property and rental units. The three crucial elements that are actually within your control, and can significantly increase your chances of finding a great deal for your first-time home purchase and the overall long-term value of that home, are: where you buy, what you buy, and how much it costs you. Of these three factors, how much it costs you is by far the most important, as that will ultimately determine how much you can make when you decide to sell it!

Fitting Your Home into Your Life

Before we can move forward with creating a wish list for your first home purchase, you will first need to estimate how long you plan to live in your home. Why? Your answer will directly impact the type, size, and location of your first home—plus your budget and mortgage terms.

As discussed in chapter 1, it is entirely possible that what you can afford now as a single woman won't be quite enough space for two or more. If you've never been married, it is not unrealistic to think that within a five- to seven-year time span you will meet a special someone for whom you will want to exchange your one-bedroom home for something bigger. If you are a recently divorced mom moving into a smaller place, finding an affordable house in a fantastic school district may be a top priority for you. Or you may have an aggressive retirement schedule—say, to stop working and retire to Florida by fifty. You may choose to move every four to five years to consecutively bigger homes as your home equity builds, to increase your net worth and have enough assets to reach Miami by the time you qualify for membership in AARP!

What goals do you have? Where do you envision yourself in five or ten years? This will have a big impact on the type of home you will be looking at. If you haven't considered this, start now! As I discussed in my first book, *Get in the Game!: The Girls' Guide to Money & Investing*, one of the easiest ways to ensure achieving your goals is to write them down. I have included a worksheet below for you to fill out about your one-year, three-year, and ten-year goals. This will help you in identifying what you are flexible about on your wish list and what is nonnegotiable when it comes to buying your first home. Start with your one-year goals first. Write five of your top goals, including buying a home. Then move on to your three-year and then your ten-year goals. The reason being that it is much easier to create the longer-term goals once you know what you are working toward in the shorter term. Don't skip this exercise, as it is a powerful tool that will only enhance you as a person and increase your chances for reaching your fullest potential—while living your life with joy, vigor, and success!

> *Your hopes, dreams, and aspirations are legitimate. They*
> *are trying to take you airborne, above the clouds, above*
> *the storms—if you will only let them!*
> *—Diane Roger*

Sample Short-Term Goals (One Year)

Buy first home
Take up a new hobby
Lose weight
Start contributing monthly to my 401(k)
Go to college
Travel
Start a business

Sample Midterm Goals (Three Years)

Buy second home
Get a new job that pays more money
Leave my boyfriend
Buy more designer shoes
Start a retirement plan
Take a year off to live in another country
Get a new car

Sample Long-Term Goals (Ten Years)

Buy third home
Quit smoking/drinking
Pay off student loans
Pay off credit card debt
Make new friends

Short–Term Goals (One Year)

1. _____

2. _____

3. _____

4. _____

5. _____

Midterm Goals (Three Years)

1. _____

2. _____

3. _____

4. _____

5. _____

Long–Term Goals (Ten Years)

1. _____

2. _____

3. _____

4. _____

5. _____

Think from Your Goals

Finally, when it comes to your goals, think *from* them, not *to* them! The biggest mistake most people make when it comes to their goals is that they view them as "over there" and see themselves traveling toward them. What makes goals the most potent and powerful is when you think *from* them! What can you actually taste, touch, smell, hear, and see when you close the door to your first home? How does it feel? The more you think from your goals, the faster you actually achieve them. The mind doesn't know the difference between real and imagined. The more you offer yourself the gift of imagining you in your first home, or any other goal for that matter, the sooner you will be in that home.

Describe Your Dream House

A wish list should be a practical and pragmatic document—it incorporates what you hope to have in your first home and what is actually reasonable to get as a first-time buyer. By asking yourself specific questions about your current lifestyle, you can more easily focus on the best location, home size, and amenities for your budget. If you prioritize the items on your list, it will be helpful not only to you, but also to your real estate agent in helping you find your first home. You should plan to make trade-offs when it comes to buying your first home. Remember, this is about purchasing your first home, not buying your dream home. By getting into your first home, you will have the opportunity to build up equity.

- **Location.** List your top three and then another two for flexibility.

- **Size.** List the ideal size and then list what you would also be open to.

- **Amenities.** List all the things you would love to have: marble bathroom, granite kitchen counter-tops, fireplace, hardwood floors, etc. Then list what is a must that you cannot do without.

- **Condition.** List what type of condition you want: move-in, fixer-upper, or newly constructed. Then list what you can work with.

As a first-time buyer, it is easy to get swept away into fantasyland about what you want to buy the first time out. The good news: By creating this reality checklist and reading this book, you are equipping yourself with important tools to help keep you grounded and focused. Don't get too caught up in perfection for your first home—remember, paying down a mortgage is infinitely financially superior to continuing to pay rent! Your goal should be to lock down that first-time home purchase and find a property that meets your needs, including: location, size, amenities, and condition. But, just as important, have the foresight to think about the next buyer's interest in the home too!

What Do You Want?

Knowing what you want and having the courage to be detailed in your description will help increase your possibility of finding that great first home fitted just for you. If you believe it is possible and are willing to do the footwork to back that belief up, chances are that not just in buying your first home, but in life too, you will get what you ask for.

You will hear often from real estate types that successful buying comes down to these three words: "location, location, location." Why? It is the one thing you absolutely can't change after you buy your home! You can decorate, remodel, paint, landscape your home . . . but if it's located next to a garbage dump, you will severely limit your chances for appreciation in property value. Think of it this way—people tend to buy "neighborhoods" as much as they buy houses. Location may also refer to the actual placement of your home within the neighborhood block it sits on. If corner lots are more valuable in your neighborhood, but your house is in the middle of the block, that is a geographic factor you will not be able to change.

Having said that, value is just as important as a factor as location. Sure, there will always be trendy neighborhoods . . . but is it really such a great idea for you to pay top dollar to buy a home in that neck of the woods if, a few years down the line, there's a new, hotter neighborhood just down the road and your 'burb will be passé? Some areas will never go out of style, but make sure you're getting a good value for what and where you're buying.

Alternatively, you may want to look for "up and coming" neighborhoods that aren't so hot right now, but may offer great possibilities for growth and property appreciation for homebuyers. Buying a home that is a good investment is one part good location and one part finding good value! Good neighborhoods will be located near, but not too near, shopping, restaurants, schools, work, transportation, and major traffic flows. They will have great amenities— maybe ocean views, beautiful green parks, wide tree-lined streets, parking, tennis courts, or quiet cul-de-sacs. You will also want to look for pride of ownership, where homeowners have wonderfully maintained their homes and landscapes. Plus, low crime rates and minimal proposed planning for local developments. Meaning: no big plans for a junkyard or overdevelopment anytime soon that could inhibit the growth of your property value. Following is a list of helpful ideas to help you research more about your prospective first-time home's neighborhood:

- Call the local planning department to find out any pertinent information on proposed planning developments.

- Call the local police department or log on to its website to check local crime rates.

- Check the local library or chamber of commerce for any newsworthy information on your prospective neighborhood.

- Drive by or walk through the neighborhood at different times of day. Chat with local residents. See what they have to say about rival neighborhoods, parking, weather, unfriendly owners, etc.

- Get an appraiser to give you a comparative analysis of the upside of home values in each neighborhood, present vs. future.

- Get your real estate agent to provide you with days-on-market (DOM) statistics. As it sounds, this research will reveal how long the average house in an area takes to sell. The shorter the time period, the greater the chance of finding a buyer at your selling price when you go to sell!

Types of Homes

There are a number of different options to choose from when it comes to finding that perfect first home. For many, the choices available to you when it comes to the different types of homes to buy will probably be automatically established up front. If you're searching for a pad in New York City, you're probably not going to find a single-family detached house! Your choices will be based on current price conditions and your ability to swing the loan with a lender to pay down a mortgage. Every type of home offers a distinctive upside and downside from a financial and personal perspective. It is important to grasp these concepts as you embark on finding a first home that is just right for your current situation.

Stand-Alone Homes

Yep, just like it sounds. These homes are the traditional-style houses that are not attached to anything else. When we ponder owning a piece of the "American Dream," most of us don't immediately conjure up a picture of a fourth floor walk-up brownstone in New York City! The two-story, white-picket-fenced home with a tall oak tree outside is still the quintessential home for many people. For this reason, the demand from buyers for stand-alone homes makes them good investments. Plus, stand-alone homes are known to appreciate quicker in value in robust property market times and be defensive in pricing during weaker times. Hence, if it is a choice between a stand-alone home and a condo, you must remember to consider these factors carefully before making your final decision.

Used vs. New

Duh. If a home has been owned before, consider it used. These types of homes tend to be less pricey than new homes. It is all about supply and demand. The fact is, there are more used homes on the market at any one given time than new homes. The supply amount equals less competition, which in turn keeps the pricing lower. Plus, property developers of new housing communities tend to be less negotiable on price, as they need to keep a set pricing standard for the entire development. Hence, you will have more flexibility in pricing with a used home too.

Another advantage of buying a used home—what you see is what you get. A used home will exist in an established neighborhood with existing parks, libraries, restaurants, and other amenities, so you can get a feel of the area right away. If you're looking at a new home in a brand-new part of town, you might be looking at nothing more than a map and a cornfield when you purchase the property. The same "what you see is what you get" advantage is also true of the carpeting, lighting, and other finishings (such as a fireplace) in an existing home. You don't have to guess at how it is going to look.

Lastly, many older homes have that elusive "charm factor." If you want molding, distinctive details, or Victorian features for your home, forget about looking at new constructions. It's in the older, used homes that you'll probably find these attractive details at an affordable price.

The downside when it comes to buying used homes is that their annual maintenance cost is overall generally higher. This is due to the simple fact that the plumbing, roof, appliances, and other components of the house are not new. All this means a fatter bill for you when it comes to maintaining the home and replacing or repairing outdated or nonworking objects. If you are seriously considering a used home, ask the owner for copies of the last several months of gas, water, sewer, and electric bills—no need to have to guesstimate at what utilities expenses you are looking at for your future home.

Is a New Home Worth It?

There is something reassuring and exciting about the idea of a new home purchase. You know that "new car smell"? Imagine how heady the "new house smell" can be. . . .

But for first-time homebuyers, buying a new home can be trickier than buying a used home. First of all, there's the cost factor. Prices on new homes tend to be less negotiable, square footage seems to be overpriced compared to that of used homes, and you may not be able to use your real estate agent, as some developers require you work with their in-house agents on-site. Also, if you're looking at a development that's not yet constructed, there's a real risk that what you end up getting may not be quite what you expected. As a novice homebuyer, I suggest you stick with finding a home that already exists!

Having said that, should you choose the new-home route, you will have the added benefit of living in a home that may have some amenities that make life more comfortable—such as more electrical outlets, no lead paint or other toxic substances, and guarantees on the life-expectancy of certain appliances and structural pieces, such as the roof. And, yes, they are generally cheaper to maintain.

Condos and Co-ops

As opposed to a stand-alone house, condos and co-ops are both, in some sense, a "shared" living situation. In order to make buying a first home a reality with your current budget, you may want to explore this type of living arrangement for your first time out of the starting gate. In fact, one out of every five first-time homebuyers buys into a condo. If this looks like a viable option to you, you will want to keep a few things to keep in mind.

Condos
First, what makes a condo a condo is not its specific design, but more importantly, how its ownership is structured. You could have a split-level townhouse condo in Orlando or a condo apartment in a Dallas high-rise. When you buy a condo, your property lines equal the interior parts of your unit—walls, floors,

ceilings, windows, and doors. You and all your condo cronies in your complex own the land and the buildings along with your units. Meaning, you all own a portion of everything outside your unit.

When you buy a condo you become a part of the homeowner's association of that project. You are not required to attend meetings, but you will be required to pay homeowner's dues for the upkeep of all the property, which is tallied up per year and divided into percentages based on the size or market value of each condo.

The upside to buying a condo is that they cost less to maintain than stand-alone homes—any costs such as landscaping/roof repairs/improvement to the entire building are split among the whole group of owners. Condos also may offer amenities (such as a swimming pool and tennis courts) that you may not be able to find in a comparably priced stand-alone home. Because they require the owner to be responsible for less upkeep, condos are an excellent choice for busy business travelers and other on-the-go types.

The downside of condos is, first, less privacy. Think of it this way, the more walls you share with your neighbors, the more noise pollution! Plus, condos are legally and financially complex. When you purchase a condo you will receive CC&Rs (Master Deed or Declaration of Covenants, Conditions, and Restrictions), the homeowner association's bylaws and budget. All of these documents are highly important and you will need to read all the fine print carefully. As for the financials, you will want to check the current operating budget for maintenance costs, staff salaries, insurance premiums, garbage collection, and all other operating expenses. Lastly, many condo projects can be "over-bearing" to say the least. The homeowners association has a lot of say regarding what you can and cannot do, including (possibly) setting strict rules about pets, allowing whether or not you can sublet your condo, controlling your freedom to make home improvements, etc. Make sure to read those bylaws and CC&Rs before you buy!

Co-ops

Just like with condos, what makes a cooperative apartment a cooperative apartment is its ownership structure.

1. **You are a co-owner and a tenant too!** When you buy a co-op, you are not actually buying the four walls that make up your apartment, as you are in a condo or a stand-alone house. In a co-op, you're actually buying into a corporation. Your mortgage purchases a specific number of shares of stock in the cooperative corporation that owns your building, and as part-owner you'll receive a stock certificate and a proprietary lease. You actually own a percentage of the company that owns your building, and you become a tenant of the building. The majority of co-ops allocate shares based on the unit size and floor location—if you have a bigger apartment, you own more shares in the company. In addition to your mortgage payment, you'll also be charged a monthly maintenance fee, which is also based upon your percentage of shares in the co-op.

2. **Co-ops have a board of directors.** If you become a member of a co-op, you will vote on the corporation's board of directors. The board is elected by you and the other members of the co-op . . . and, in fact, you can actually try to get elected to the board if you want to have a larger hand in the running of your building. Think of the board as a similar structure to the condo's homeowners association, in that it is responsible for the managing of the building.

3. **Co-ops have some financial hurdles.** Some lenders flat out refuse to accept shares of a corporation as security for a mortgage, meaning it might be tougher for you to get a mortgage to buy a co-op. Also, co-op boards are notoriously picky about who they allow into a building and their financial requirements. Most co-ops are found in New York City; outside of that area, you might find it tough to finance your purchase of a co-op.

For this last reason alone, you will most likely not be exploring a co-op situation as a first-time homebuyer unless you're located in New York City or a few other major metropolitan areas.

Fixer-Upper

For some of us, finding an affordable home might mean having to make some trade-offs. A fixer-upper can be a great deal if you're handy and don't mind tackling a few projects to get your dream home into top shape. But you want to be sure you know what you're signing on for. There's a big difference between a *Trading Spaces*–style spruce-up and *The Money Pit*. If you want to make sure a fixer-upper is a good deal for you, you will want to take extra special care to work with a great property inspector (which we will discuss in the next chapter), and get a fair market price for the property to ensure that you can make a profit when you choose to sell it after the "fixing-up" phase has taken place. You will also want to try to find and buy the cheapest house on the block in the best neighborhood you can afford. Fixer-uppers are notorious for costing more than you bargained for, taking longer than you expected, and generally being hassle-filled—at minimum. Be careful to think through this decision before you leap into buying a fixer-upper!

What Kinds of Renovations Are Doable?

Technically speaking, renovations should help increase the actual value of a home by making it more functional and pleasant to live in. Such renovations could be, a new garage, an updated kitchen, or an added-on bathroom. You also have cosmetic value, which includes landscaping, carpeting, painting, etc. Cosmetic renovations also increase the value of a home and are actually much easier to make.

Keep in mind, structural repairs to a home are *not* renovations; they are changes that you make to be in accordance with local health and safety standards. Good examples include new electrical, plumbing, foundation repairs, roof replacements, etc. Be extra careful, as these structural repairs tend to be very pricey yet add little value to a home. It is not unusual to have the seller address some of this work prior to buying the home. The idea being, the less you spend on structural repairs for your fixer-upper, the more you have to spend for renovations. If the cost estimates you receive on your fixer-upper will land your house as the most expensive on the block, forget about it.

Paying for Renovations

As a general rule, acquiring a loan from a lender for up to 3 percent of the property value to apply to the renovations for your fixer-upper is a good benchmark, acquiring a loan from a lender beyond 3 percent of the property value to apply to the renovations for your fixer-upper will be challenging. However, your mortgage broker will probably know of a few lenders who may specialize in offering those types of loans. If the lender finds you and your project creditworthy, they may offer you beyond the 3 percent for your required construction loan.

Square Footage

Before we create your reality wish list for your first home, you need to be in the know about square feet. When you shop for your first home, you will see on the listing sheet the square footage of the home. One square foot equals a square that is one foot by one foot. So if you have a 20 x 20 room, that equals two hundred square feet.

Be cautious about believing square footage estimates that may be provided to you by the seller. Why? Because calculating square feet is often done by using the exterior perimeter of the house rather than by measuring the actual interior living space. You technically lose a lot of square feet to walls, closets, chimney vents, plumbing, etc. As in any other sale, selling brokers want to create the best possible listing sheet to sell their property for their client. It is not unrealistic to think that a house with 2,000 square feet could actually be listed as one with 2,500 square feet (New York City apartments are notorious for this type of square-footage inflation). If you want the real numbers, either ask the owners for an architectural plan or measure the interior perimeter yourself.

How to Remember Each Home

You will need to create a method that allows you to accurately remember all the key features of each home you see. It is not unusual to think that you will be seeing at minimum ten homes. And after the first five, it is easy to begin confusing which house had what feature. Plus, keeping good records allows you to do your own comparative analysis of what is out there and what is the best deal available to you given your specifications.

As you embark on the open-house circuit, you will want to keep a journal with the date of the showing, the brokers involved, and any attached listing sheets and information for each house. Make notes on the listing sheets of things you found memorable about the home, size, price, amenities, or even number of bedrooms or bathrooms. Take pictures or even video footage of the homes you see. The more detailed information you gather, the easier it will be to make a final decision as to what will work best for you given your allowance and what is actually available in that price range.

The Educated Buyer

In an effort to help you operate as an educated buyer who has the ability to determine the true value of a home and red flag overpriced homes, to keep you from getting a raw deal on your first home, here are a few simple concepts to keep in mind and apply when the situation presents itself.

Understanding Fair Market Value

In essence, fair market value is the price a seller is willing to accept and a buyer is willing to pay for a house. Fair market value is powerful in that it conveys the idea that a home will always sell for the right price. You see, you as the buyer will have your idea of what the house is worth and the seller will have their idea of what the sales price of the house should be. When a seller and a buyer agree to a price, it becomes fair market value, a true bankable fact of what the mutually acceptable price is. Given that we are in a hot property cycle due to low interest rates and robust price appreciation in homes, sellers have had great opportunities to establish in bankable fact what their idea of the correct fair market value should be. Don't get too entangled in the web of what the current seller bought his house for and how unfair to sell at such an obscenely fat profit. It will be a waste of your and everyone else's time. Fair market value is in a sense excruciatingly un-encumbered by both the seller and the buyer because it does not care how much the seller needs to make on the sale because they overpaid when they bought it and need to recover their remodeling expenses, pay off their loan, or buy their next home.

The Skinny on Median Sale Prices

Median sale prices absolutely don't give you fair market value for a home! Median sale price numbers are produced by organizations such as the chamber of commerce or even the National Association of Realtors for a targeted geographic area in a city, county, or state for home sales activity. At the current writing of this book, median sale prices for homes in America are at $140,000. Meaning, half of the homes sold for $140,000 or more and half sold below $140,000. This number does not reveal what type of homes, the square footage, land included, etc. In fact, you don't even know which part of America it is referring to! The only two pieces of helpful information for you in median numbers is the reference to historical median prices vs. the present, to help you see the percentage increase per annum. If it was $100,000 five years ago and $140,000 now, well that is 40 percent apprecia-tion in five years, not too shabby of an investment re-turn. The second is comparability in price from one city to another. If median prices are at $200,000 in L.A., but $50,000 in Phoenix—you know how much more mileage your dollars will get you in Phoenix than in L.A.

Getting the Real Picture on Prices

Once you get serious about a possible first home purchase, you will want to ask your real estate agent to prepare a written comparable market analysis (CMA). The CMA on any given home will offer you a comparable analysis of other homes (*comps* in real estate jargon—meaning, *comparable prices*) located in the same neighborhood that are similar in size, age, and condition and have sold in the past six months. CMAs are truly the most accurate way to reflect local property market conditions, which are determined by mortgage rates, business conditions, and consumer confidence. Suffice it to say, if property prices are on a decline, you will find asking prices today in the market lower than what is on the sheet of comps. Conversely, if property prices are on the rise, you will find comps on the sheet lower than asking prices today. Lastly, sale prices on these CMAs are much more important than asking prices, which at this point should be obvious to you given your new knowledge of fair market values!

The Importance of Appraisals

As mentioned earlier, a final way to determine the value of a home from an expert with an unbiased opinion is to hire an appraiser. Although appraisals are an extra cost of a few hundred bucks (and they can be time-consuming, due to the fact that the appraiser inspects the property meticulously from top to bottom), it is a great way to get a second opinion as a first-time homebuyer to reassure you of a your potential home's value. Remember, an appraiser, unlike your real estate agent, has no vested interest in making the deal happen—this could ultimately save you big bucks. The last thing you want to find after all your hard work is that you overpaid for a home.

Now that you are "in the know" and have a clearer picture of what you are looking for in your first home purchase, how to begin looking for that home, what the fair market value is—both present and future—and what types of repair/renovation work you will want to do on your future home, it is time to make an offer.

8

How Do I Negotiate the Best Deal Possible?

Deciding What to Offer, How to Offer, and Closing the Deal Like Donald Trump

If you think you are beaten, you are,
If you think you dare not, you don't.
If you like to win, but you think you can't,
It is almost certain you won't
—Napoleon Hill

As a finance professional, Betty is a confident negotiator. She implicitly understands that not all deals work out and that the market does not always go your way. But that was sometimes tough to remember as she was looking for a home. Betty was outbid on eight different properties in New York City over a period of six months, and began to despair of ever finding a home of her own.

However, Betty also appreciated the principle that "persistence overcomes resistance." She had done her homework and trusted that she would finally prevail—which she did. After eight false starts, Betty is now the proud owner of a co-op in Brooklyn Heights and says that she is glad none of those other deals worked out because she absolutely loves her first "owned" home!

* * *

The last few weeks and months have been busy ones. You have sorted out your financial budget, found a mortgage broker, gotten preapproved for a loan, secured a fantastic real estate agent, put together a reality wish list, and started exploring houses and neighborhoods via the Internet—all of which puts you in a great position to know what is being offered in the marketplace, and how much it costs. Now you're nearly ready for the final negotiation process: making an offer and closing escrow on your first home purchase.

When it comes to buying your first home, one of the most competitive edges you can have in the negotiating process is *time*. Most sellers are motivated by life changes—weddings, retirement, job relocation, expanding family, death, or deadlines with escrow on a new property they are buying. If you, as the prospective buyer, are not under any pressure from your end of the deal, you're in a strong negotiating position. The majority of negotiations finalize in the last hour or even minutes before the deadline. If you are negotiating from a place of strength, you have the opportunity to improve your deal right up until the very end.

Real estate tycoons like Donald Trump have proven time and again that they truly think with a "billionaire mindset" when it comes to successfully negotiating real estate deals. You can, too, if you can get your mind around a few straightforward negotiation tips. Wheel and deal like the master!

Two Trump-like Negotiation Tips

1. *Keep Your Emotions in Check with a Healthy Perspective*

> *I have noticed that nothing I never said*
> *ever did me any harm.*
> —Calvin Coolidge

Moving, in and of itself, is estimated to be one of the top five most stressful experiences we can go through. Combine that with plunking down the biggest chunk of change you've ever spent in your life, and watch your anxiety levels soar. It's OK to get emotional and stressed during this process. Heck, if you're not freaking out a little, you probably don't have a pulse. But ultimately, you have to think of this as a business transaction and not get too emotionally invested in any one property. If you can recognize this as you are entering into your negotiation process, you will have a much better chance of managing yourself and getting the best deal possible.

Until all parties sign on the dotted line, your deal isn't done! Keeping your emotions in check with a healthy distance while your real estate transaction is being negotiated and processed is a very holistic approach. It is sort of like dating—cautiously optimistic, but if it doesn't work out, you get to practice knowing that it wasn't meant to be and that there truly is something even better for you out there.

2. Keep It Real

You want to keep a realistic perspective of what is available to you in your price range and continue to grow in your ability to accurately appreciate what the market has to offer. Don't fantasize that you are going to get your first home today for yesterday's prices, or that you will necessarily be able to afford a house similar to your childhood home. The more you delve into your home search and review your CMAs with your real estate agent, the more you will begin to understand. Good deals and bad deals are made each day. The more you know, the better chance you have of operating as an educated buyer who can find an affordable house at a good price.

Making the Offer

Making money is art and working is art and good
business is the best art of all.
—Andy Warhol

Once you find that potential "right" first house for you, it will be time to take your next step by making an offer to purchase. Your real estate agent will help you put together a purchase contract—a fairly standard agreement that is revised on an ongoing basis to ensure that new real estate laws are reflected. Each state's is different, and you will want to check to make sure you are working off the most current one with your real estate agent.

You want to stay in tune with the fact that the object of this contract is to buy what you want, let the seller sell what he wants, and in the process make sure you both get what you want. Good offers to purchase have that exact purpose by offering the seller a reality-based offering price. This price will be calculated based off of your CMAs, appraisal of the property (which we discussed in the previous chapter), and your real estate agent's input.

Your offer will also need to include pragmatic financing terms from your lender that reflect current market lending conditions when it comes to your interest rate on the loan, loan amount, loan-origination fee, timing, etc. This, too, is where being preapproved for a loan truly makes your offer go from good to great! Sellers know you are serious and that you can deliver the deal that you promise.

Lastly, great offers don't ask for money up front to address potential property defects. Remember, this is a negotiation process, and your first goal with submission of your offer to purchase contract is to get your offer accepted by the seller. Your offer to purchase contract will also include important property inspection clauses that are known as contingencies, that in essence will allow you to reenter into negotiations when it comes to any vital corrective work after property inspection reports are received.

What Now?

Once your offer has been actually accepted and property inspectors have determined what specific corrective work is required, you and the seller will then resume your negotiations equipped with these technical facts. In this scenario, you save time in the negotiation process by not arguing about how much the corrective work will cost until you have the hard facts, thereby upping your chances for the seller to accept paying in full for the corrective work to be done!

Smart Negotiations

As mentioned in the beginning of this chapter, negotiating is an ongoing process. Expect that you will get a counter offer from the seller. Sellers make counter offers so that they can tweak the price, terms, and conditions to their best fit. If it comes down to a standstill between a sum of a few thousand dollars, offer to split the difference 50-50. Normally, those few thousand dollars would only equal 1–2 percent of a home's fair market value. It is a way to make the deal work for both you, the buyer, and the seller, ultimately making it a win-win situation. You want to think of yourself as a negotiator who is working together with the seller to find solutions that are satisfactory to both sides.

Keep Contingencies Simple!

A contingency is some specific future event that must be satisfied in order for the sale of a property to go through. Meaning, a contingency gives you the right to pull out of a deal if that event fails to happen. Beyond your property inspection contingencies, your offer to purchase contract will also contain other important escape clauses. Standard contingencies include: your right to review and approve the property's title report or review the master deed bylaws and budget. Plus, other standard contingencies that could sour a deal would be that inspection reports are not up to your snuff or you can't ultimately get your financing from your lender. You will want to keep your contingencies as simple as possible, especially in a seller's market. Too many contingencies mean too many ways in which the potential deal on the table can fall through. Most contracts include the financing and inspection contingencies as a given. Ultimately, you must protect yourself, while also having the seller accept your offer—a delicate balancing act that any fine female such as yourself can handle!

Make Your Offer Attractive

As of this writing, as you all know by now, interest rates are low and the housing market is hot, hot, hot! Homes newly listed on the market quickly generate multiple offers. If you want to increase your chances of going to the top of the pile and ultimately have the seller accept your offer to purchase, you will first want to keep your emotions out of the driver's seat. Use your comparable market data and the expert opinion of your real estate agent to decide together the top limit you are prepared to pay for the house. Decide your limit, and stick to it! Don't get swept up in a moment of passion for this property.

Think about the seller for a minute. Your seller is looking for the best price, terms, and contingencies of sale. You can sweeten the deal by finding out what exactly the seller is looking for . . . and it may not even be more money! Some sellers find big down payments attractive, as they feel that this guarantees you will get financing. Others appreciate the opportunity to have a long escrow period in order to find another home. Perhaps you can offer to purchase the house "as-is"— based, of course, on approval of inspection (just in the case the house is a money pit). And, as mentioned earlier, your preapproval by a lender is a bonus for you when making an offer too.

Forget the Lowball Offers

By now in your negotiation process, you are getting a good Trump-like taste for well-priced properties vs. grossly overpriced houses. Your goal as a nice negotiator is to make a fair offer on your first home based off of comparable house prices. By lowballing, you buck this trend immediately and kill any chance of establishing a good rapport with the seller that would offer you both the chance of smooth win-win negotiations. As a barometer, going below a fifth of what the house is worth, or 20 percent, probably won't work unless the seller is desperate. Plus, who wants to move into a home that could be filled with all that bad juju to begin with!

Keep in mind, a low offer is not a lowball offer. If you offer $137,500 for a $150,000 listed property but comparable houses in that area are selling for are between $135,000 and $150,000, you are, in fact, at the low-end range of fair market value—but your offer is not, in fact, a lowball offering. Sellers tend to anticipate that buyers never pay asking price—hence, they leave room to negotiate. While buyers who jibe

Should I Offer in Writing, or in Person?

Get your agent to make your offer in person. It is too easy to say no over the phone and leaves little room to negotiate. Get your agreement in writing. The spoken word as an agreement means nothing in a court of law. Keeping log notes with dates, times, and what was said can only help in your negotiation process too!

with property market values tend to make their initial offer price on the low side to offer themselves room to negotiate too!

The Home Inspection

It is estimated that 40 percent of houses have at least one major defect, and since a house's value is directly affected by its physical condition, you will need to take an extremely cautious approach when it comes to reviewing exactly what corrective work is needed on your future first-home purchase. Believe it or not, you have the opportunity to make a few good inspections yourself to review with your future property inspector. First, you can perform basic inspection tests like flushing toilets, flipping light switches, turning the stove on and off, checking the water pressure by turning water on, looking for leaky faucets, and checking inside the fridge to see if it holds cold air. These simple tests may uncover more repairs than expected. After all, you will want all these basics to function properly upon move in.

More heightened corrective repairs to look for include:

- **Smelly.** If the basement feels damp and/or is smelly, that could be a sign of leakage or molding.

- **Sticky.** Doors, windows, skylights, etc., should open and close easily and with precision.

- **Spots.** Check walls and ceiling for spots that may indicate a water leakage problem from the roof, walls, or pipes.

- **Structural.** Check to make sure floors and walls are even. Floors don't slope and walls don't bulge.

- **Sloppy electrical or masonry work.** Do-it-yourself patch-up jobs could indicate bigger problems down the road for you. Look for messy electrical boxes and any unusual-looking repair jobs.

- **Insects.** If your future first home is made of wood or stucco, make sure to look along all areas of the property that touch the earth, such as garage, foundation, deck, etc. Mud tubes along the foundation or in the basement indicate termite infestation.

You should plan to have both yourself and the seller present during inspections. It is a heck of a lot easier to negotiate with the seller once the inspection reports arrive if they have, in fact, been witness to the damage that needs to be repaired with their own eyes. Believe it or not, the big "yeah" or "nah" during the property negotiation process is when you finally meet with the seller to negotiate corrective work credits for the property. As you can imagine, many sellers don't want to pay up for the work to be done and obviously you as a buyer don't either. With corrective work, the value of a house is diminished until the work has been completed. If a house is listed for $250,000, along with other comparable houses with no termites or dry rot, solid foundations, and good roofs, then the seller needs to fully appreciate that the new listing price, after inspection, for their house will be lower. In this example, the originally listed home for $250,000, with an estimated amount of $30,000 of corrective work, will have a new listing price of $220,000. If the seller refuses to lower the price or address the corrective work, you may need to withdraw from the deal.

It is ultimately in the interest of the seller to save time and work out a deal with you, as any future buyers will need to have what you discovered disclosed to them, which will ultimately lower the price of the home in any event.

Lenders do get involved when there is major corrective work to be done. Especially when the loan-to-value ratio on the home is more than 80 percent. It is not unusual for lenders to review the inspection reports too! Normally, the sellers leave ample funds in escrow to cover the required corrective costs, the lender holds the full corrective amount in a savings account until the corrective work has been completed, or sellers may give a credit for corrective work directly to buyers at the close of escrow to offset their loan origination fees, which include: appraisal, loan points, credit report, title insurance, and property inspections.

Finding One Good Property Inspector

Once you have an accepted offer and before you remove your inspection contingencies on your contract, you will need to find a good property inspector who can perform a full prepurchase interior and exterior components inspection. The inspection will cover all areas of the property, including plumbing, electrical, heating and cooling systems, smoke detectors, foundation, kitchen, bathrooms, roof and gutters, and health and safety hazards. This inspection will cost you anywhere from $300 to $500 and up, depending on where you live. Don't scrimp on this expense, as it is one of the important costs you will need to incur before signing on the dotted line of your big fat mortgage contract.

Most states don't require property inspectors to be certified or licensed to inspect homes—so you might get some contractor masquerading as an inspector offering to make the repairs. Smells fishy, no? Can anyone say, conflict of interest? Good property inspectors make their living solely from performing property inspections. Plus, good property inspectors hold licenses or certifications in their field. A well-known professional association of home inspectors that may be useful to you is the American Society of Home Inspectors. All ASHI members are certified and have performed 250 property inspections, at minimum, plus they are required to pass two written proficiency exams prior to acceptance of membership. They are on the Web at www.ashi.com or can be reached at 800-743-2744.

Make sure your property inspector confirms how long the inspection will take, that you and the seller can tag along at the time of inspection, and that they are happy to offer referral numbers for you to call. You will also want to clarify when you will receive the written inspection report. These days, many property inspectors use handheld computers during the inspection tour, which they then use to print copies for you and the seller after the inspection is finished. Get a quote for the inspection job. Don't fall prey to the coupon inspection special of the week. In fact, if your property inspector offers you one, question their inspection capabilities right then and there! Due to market competition, good property inspector rates tend to be comparable.

Finally, when you receive your inspection report make sure it accurately reflects the defects your inspector or even you pointed out during the inspection. Chances are you will have a few corrective repairs, hopefully less vs. more. You will want to use licensed contractors only to bid for the job—and use your property inspector as an ally during the bidding process. Property inspectors can answer in more detail any questions contractors could have about the corrective repair work, and in some cases property inspectors make themselves available for an additional fee to evaluate bids you receive for the work.

Going Back to the Second "I" of PITI

The rules are simple, you put less than 20 percent of the purchase price down for a home and you will be required to have homeowners insurance by your lender. When you review the insurance policy, you will want to look for a few critical elements to protect yourself. For one, find out in the dwelling coverage section what specifically it says under the guaranteed replacement cost provision. As you may have guessed, this replacement is referring to the worst-case scenario: your future first home burning to the ground and the actual cost to rebuild it! You want a policy that insures that if the cost to rebuild your fire-savaged home is more than the estimated value in the contract, that the insurers will still cough up the difference in change.

Second, make sure your lawsuit protection is at least two times the value of your assets. This protection is called an umbrella or an excess-liability policy, which helps insure you against lawsuits from others who may incur an unusual accident while on your property. This coverage can be bought in increments of $1 million and actually adds to the liability coverage on your home and car too!

Lastly, under your personal property protection, which is normally determined by the actual total coverage amount of the property, normally 50–75 percent of that number, you will want to ask for a rider (*add on*), if it isn't a normal part of your insurance contract, in which you request a personal property replacement guarantee. As this type of insurance actually replaces the cost of an item stolen or damaged vs. the cost of it at insurance time. Remember to take photos or video footage of all your items; it could be extremely helpful in the future should the worst happen to you.

Discounts for the Second "I" of your PITI!

Now that you are in the know as to what to look for when shopping for your homeowners insurance, you will want to shop around for an insurer who can offer you the best deal. By putting a little legwork into this part of the process, you will potentially find premiums that are 35–50 percent less than others. A few direct writers of homeowners insurance include: American Express (800-535-2001), Amica (800-242-6422), Erie Insurance Group (800-458-0811), Geico (800-841-3000), and USAA (800-531-8100). Plus, check your phone book for local listings of agents who sell: Liberty Mutual, State Farm, and Nationwide Mutual policies. Ask about special promotions, discounts for new roofs or even security systems, multiple coverage, being a nonsmoker, or other creative ways they may offer to help you achieve the lowest-rate quote possible given your specific insurance requirements.

Title Insurance?

Yep, you will also need title insurance to protect yourself in case someone makes a claim to ownership after you have bought the property. Sounds crazy, right? In fact, approximately 90 percent of your title insurance monies will be spent up front to determine who exactly legally owns the property you are looking to buy. Plus, seek to uncover any unpaid tax liens or judgments recorded against it. The last 10 percent of your title insurance monies will go toward protecting you against any future claims on your property's title after escrow closes. You can expect one piece of good news from this insurance, and possibly a second. The first piece of good news is that title insurance is a one-time fee to be paid at the close of escrow. Second, depending on which state you buy property in, the seller may be required to pay for it, or split it between the two of you. In some cases, though, you end up paying for it yourself. But unless you refinance your mortgage down the road, you will not be required to make this payment again for the life of your mortgage.

Exercising in Escrow

Finally, your *escrow*—a word that is often kicked around when discussing real estate, and one that you may have only pretended to understand up until this point. What is escrow *really*?

Once you and your seller have a signed contract (*ratified offer* in real estate jargon), all VIP documents, monies, and specific instructions on how to carry out the deal will need to be delivered to an escrow officer. Why? Technically speaking, your escrow officer is a neutral third party who acts on both your and the seller's behalf, while the two of you work out the finer details of the deal. The simple act of delivering these documents to your escrow holder officially enacts the escrow. As mentioned earlier, just because you are in escrow does *not* mean that you have the house. Not until you have the final closing bill in your hands do you truly own the home. Until then, anything is fair game, and the chances of falling out of escrow are good in a seller's market, so buyer beware!

The escrow officer that you and the seller agree to choose could be a title company, a lawyer, or even an escrow firm. Your real estate agent will most likely make a few recommendations for you. Make sure to check the fee structure and check them out for their service quality.

As we discussed earlier, your contract will be filled with contingencies that will need to be met before you approve the sale, such as property inspection re-ports. Another alternative contingency issue would be if your seller is unable to give you clear title to the property. If you ultimately do not find these reports or alternative issues acceptable, you have the option to instruct the escrow officer to not give any monies to the seller before you are fully satisfied that your seller has performed under the contract.

Escrow Officer Official Exercises

Your escrow officer's role is to receive your instructions and abide by them. Should your escrow officer receive instructions that don't jibe between you and the seller, the escrow comes to one big halt until the discrepancy is resolved. Common issues that arise include: repair work taking place prior to or after escrow, and personal property items such as the fridge staying or going, etc. Make it a point to be diplomatic if this worst-case scenario does arise, and try to keep a cool head with the bigger picture in mind. Taking the time to befriend your escrow officer is a good way to go too! Checking to see if you could provide any additional information or assist them in their process can only help you when you are exercising in escrow.

Taxes, Liens, and Property Restrictions

Shortly after your escrow opens, you will receive a preliminary title report, which proves who owns the actual property and if there are any taxes or liens against the property and third party restrictions that could limit the use of your potential property. This VIP document is not title insurance in and of itself. You will want to review your preliminary title report with your agent, title representative, or even escrow officer. You will have the right from your contract to reasonably disapprove of paying certain claims or restrictions on the property before taking ownership. In this situation, the owner will need to clear them prior to the close of escrow.

The Final Bill Please!

You will want to check with your escrow officer, at the opening of escrow, to determine exactly how much your total bill will be at close of escrow. Don't feel ashamed of scraping your nickels together to make closing costs, as buyers are always known to be notoriously short of funds when purchasing a home. You may find that it may take a few weeks to get an itemization of your bill, which will include your homeowners insurance premiums, inspection fees, corrective work credits, etc. However, having a preliminary itemized bill is certainly something to begin with and plan for as all these final numbers come rolling in the door. When you walk into your closing, have your checkbook ready, and consult with your escrow officer about how you can pay. You will need a money order, cashier's check, or bank-wired funds just prior to the close. Overestimate your final closing costs and plan appropriately.

Your Credit and Debit Statement

Once you actually close on your house, you will receive that very day a final closing statement, which itemizes the final bill of the house purchase in a credit and debit fashion. Meaning, credits are any/all monies to put toward your home purchase, such as a deposit, down payment, or even credit from the seller for corrective work or unpaid property taxes. These credits show up in your account balance as a credit to you. Debits are monies that are taken out of escrow for payments on your behalf, such as the price of your first home purchase, loan fees, property inspection fees, and homeowners insurance. Luckily, you will have the opportunity to meet with your escrow officer a few days before the scheduled closing and you will be given a preliminary closing statement to review. This is the one huge bill that you will need to review extremely carefully. Check meticulously line by line to ensure that it is correct! Remember to keep a copy of this bill safeguarded—it will come in extra handy at tax time, as your loan origination fees and property tax payments will be deductible. Plus, when you go to sell the property for that bigger, better house in a few years, you will need this bill to establish any taxes owed at that time for the monies you made off of the property from the time you first bought it. But, don't forget, as we discussed in chapter 1, after two years, any profits you make are all yours, free and clear of Uncle Sam!

Making a Move

Just as you will get a preliminary closing bill a few days before close, you will also want to plan to visit your new future first home a few days before closing to ensure the house is in the same general condition as when you agreed to make an offer to purchase it. Most standard real estate contracts have clauses that offer you this option. Technically, you don't own your home till the day after escrow closes—when the escrow officer calls to tell you that the seller has received his monies, the deed has been recorded, and they inform you, "YOU GOT THE HOUSE!" As for actually making the big move to take possession, read the contract clause titled "Closing and Occupancy." Keep your life simple; don't try to move in on the day your escrow closes. If you negotiate to sign a rent-back agreement with the seller whereby they rent the property back from you after close for a brief time before moving to their own greener pastures, then you can expect them to pay your total monthly payment for the house prorated for the time they are there, which will include the full amount of your monthly PITI. Lastly, if the house is vacant before escrow closes and you have an urge to begin making minor fix-ups to the place, resist. If the deal falls through in escrow, you are left with a loss of time, money, and a few sorrows to boot!

Refund Please!

May we be content with our lot, which when you think about it, is quite a lot.
—*Unknown*

So, you did it! You made your first home purchase happen and you are filled with that achy feeling that you got a crap mortgage, that you overpaid for the house, and that property prices are about to tank. Not to mention the fact that you feel intense job insecurity and a healthy panic attack coming down the pike all at the same time.

Chill. Your feelings are normal, and the majority of homebuyers go through this initial phase of self-doubt. Welcome to the world of real estate ownership, dear! Make a cup of tea, go for a long walk, journal, and talk to a good friend or close family member, and keep in mind—this too shall pass.

In not too short of a time you will come to realize that relatively speaking, in the bigger picture, you did a great job with your mortgage negotiations, property prices will go up, you still are gainfully employed, and in optimal health.

Finally, congratulations for stepping up to the plate. I celebrate your courage to be big and create the opportunity to build wealth, security, and a high quality of life for yourself. Kudos to you! *Viva La Casa!*

Resources for Homebuyers

Books

Glink, Ilyce R. *100 Questions Every First-Time Home Buyer Should Ask, second edition,* Three Rivers Press: 2000.

Irwin, Robert. *Home Buyer's Checklist,* McGraw-Hill: 2001.

————. *How to Buy a Home When You Can't Afford It,* McGraw-Hill: 2002.

Mclean, James Andrew. *The Home Buyer's Advisor,* John Wiley & Sons: 2004.

Mungo, Ray and Robert Yamaguchi. *No Credit Required,* Penguin: 1993.

Tyson, Eric and Ray Brown. *Mortgages for Dummies, second edition,* For Dummies: 2004.

Websites

www.coldwellbanker.com, www.century21.com, and *www.remax.com.* National real estate agents.

www.cyberhomes.com. Almost all homes for sale are listed on the Internet; this is another good site to research houses for sale.

www.fanniemaefoundation.org/ and *www.freddiemac.com/*. Good places to check out low-interest, minimal-money-down financing, and special programs geared for first-time homebuyers.

www.mortgage.com, www.quicken.com, www.eloan.com, and *www.lendingtree.com.* Good mortgage sites to get a sense of current rates and different lenders available to you.

www.realtor.com. The official site for the National Association of Realtors®, this site offers useful statistics, tons of helpful information, and a generic mortgage calculator.

About the Author

Vanessa Summers is a television host, motivational speaker, and author of, *Get in the Game! The Girls' Guide to Money & Investing* (Bloomberg Press, 2001). She is also a registered investment adviser with the Department of Corporations in the State of California. *Glamour* magazine named her the "Money Model" and Mark Haine's of CNBC's *Squawk Box* refers to Vanessa as the "Financial Guru of the MTV generation." Vanessa's on-air guest appearances include: Fox News—*Your World with Neil Cavuto*, CBS's—*The Early Show*, NBC's—*The Early Today Show*, CNNfn's—*The Money Gang & Business Unusual*, Bloomberg's—*Personal Finance*, CNBC's *Squawk Box,* and CNBC's *Street Signs* with Maria Bartiromo, and MSNBC's—*Economy Watch*.

Summers resides in Los Angeles, where she recently shot her first network television pilot for VH-1 and teaches a four-week "Wealth & Success" workshop on how to ignite your moneymaker from within, in Beverly Hills with her partner, Andor Gyulai, who is an investment consultant. For more information or to sign-up for her free monthly "Wealth & Success Warrior" newsletter, please log on to: www.vanessasummers.com.

As a young teen, her career began as a top-ranked USTA tennis player in Florida where she competed regularly against Jennifer Capriatti, Arancha Sanchez Viccario, and Mary Jo Fernandez. Vanessa then embarked on her second career in New York City as a fashion model, where she was represented by the Ford Management Group at age seventeen. She went on to become a sales trader in Hong Kong at age twenty-three with a top-tier brokerage firm named Jardine Fleming before moving back to the United States in 1998 to become the head of Sales and Marketing for a women's fund.

In the beginning of 2000, out of a deep desire and passion to help other young women conquer their own money trail, she founded and currently serves as Chief Adventure Officer of the Sutra Foundation (www.sutrafoundation.com): an education-based nonprofit that seeks to motivate, inspire, and educate young women to get started with their money, investing, and planning for financial freedom.

Index

Page numbers in *italic* indicate illustrations.